The Bride of Jesus

A glorious church awaiting the return of the Lord

CAROL NKAMBULE

Copyright © CAROL NKAMBULE

All rights reserved. No part of this book may be reproduced or transmitted in any form or by any means, electronic or mechanical, including photocopying, recording or any information storage or retrieval system without permission from the copyright holder.

The author has made every effort to trace and acknowledge sources/resources/individuals. In the event that any images/information have been incorrectly attributed or credited, the author will be pleased to rectify these omissions at the earliest opportunity.

Unless otherwise stated all scripture quotations have been taken from the New King James Version (NKJV) of the Bible.

ISBN 978-0-6399523-0-7

eISBN 978-0-6399523-1-4

Published by Author using Kingdom Anchored publishing services,

P O Box 3794, Nelspruit, 1200.

Edited by J Mqamelo, proof read by M Raphasha

Cover Designed by Carol Nkambule

Interior designed by Bathabile Kutu

Website: www.carolnkambule.co.za or

www.kingdomanchored.co.za

Email – carolnkambule@gmail.com

Dedication

To the saints, the Bride in Waiting, the beloved of the Lord God. This is a call for the refueling of our lamps so that they may shine brighter.

To my husband, for your patience while I spent time on this assignment, your reward is with God.

To my children – my prayer is that I will stand alongside you all before the Lord when He comes.

To my parents – I love you. Thank you for supporting me.

To my sister and prayer partner – may God grant you the desires of your heart.

To my brothers – my hands are always raised up to the Lord for you.

CONTENTS

Introduction	i
The Bridegroom	1
Chosen	8
Given by the Father	19
The bride price is paid	25
Follows her husband	40
Intimate	61
Pursues holiness	76
Submits	88
Cared for	97
Empowered	106
Must be ready	116
Glorious	122
Manifests the Lord	128
Loved	137

Mature	**149**
Grounded in the Word	**166**
Positioned to influence	**179**
The bride	**191**
Author's parting words	**202**

Introduction

'Let us be glad and rejoice and give Him glory, for the marriage of the Lamb has come, and His wife has made herself ready. And to her it was granted to be arrayed in fine linen, clean and bright, for the fine linen is the righteous acts of the saints'

(Revelation 19:7–8).

A wedding is a beautiful and joyous occasion. It is a time of celebration, a joining together of two families, and the beginning of a lasting union between two souls. There is a feast, whether big or small. Many come together to publicly celebrate the love of the couple, and to wish them well. That day is the first step of a lifetime commitment.

The two main characters in a wedding are the bride and the groom. The bride arrayed in her beautiful dress is always beautiful. These days, makeup artists and hair stylists make even those with less than perfect looks appear radiant and beautiful.

The bride is thoroughly prepared for this day, and makes every effort to look flawless in the eyes of her husband – for it is he she wants to impress, more than those looking on.

The preparation of the bride is well portrayed in the book of Esther. When the king wanted a queen, many virgins were brought to the palace and prepared for him. The girls went through a twelve-month preparation period. Scripture tell us that for six months Esther was prepared with oils of myrrh, and six months with other perfumes for the beautifying of women (Esther 2:12). These oils removed all sorts of blemishes, dealing with any skin problems that might have been present. Finally Esther was presented as a perfect and radiant bride to the king.

I have seen many grooms break down and cry when they see their bride approach. He looks at her with the eyes that say, 'She is mine!' She looks to him and is glad to see that he approves of her. She wants to look the best she can, and it is all for him.

The Greek word used in Revelation to describe the Church is *gyne*, meaning bride or wife. The word indicates that a wedding is to come. The Lamb has given himself to His bride.

The Bible tells us that a day will come for the wedding feast. *'Blessed are those who are called to the mar-*

riage supper of the Lamb' (Revelation 19:9).

What a joyous occasion it will be. The invitation is out, extended to all who accept the bridegroom, who say 'Yes' to Jesus. It will be too late to accept the invitation on the day of the wedding, the proposal cannot be accepted then. Those who accept the proposal go immediately into preparation mode, awaiting the day of the wedding.

According to the custom of the ancient Middle East, the setting in which the Bible was written, the wedding took place in three stages. First, the parents chose a bride for the groom, just as God calls the elect out of the world to be the bride of Christ through salvation and regeneration. In the second stage, the groom goes to the home of the bride, accompanied by his friends, to escort her from her home to his – just as Christ will come to take His bride at the rapture. In the third stage, the wedding feast is held at the groom's home, lasting for several days. We, too, will celebrate with the Lord when He comes, and our joy will know no end.

This book is an intimate discourse on the Church, reflecting on the upcoming wedding. A wedding requires preparation and readiness. Once a bride accepts the proposal for marriage, she begins to prepare. She envisions her day, the colour scheme, the dress, the hair, the suit of her husband, the décor, the venue, the guests and many more details on her 'to do' list. The Church, as the bride of Jesus, is also in preparation mode. She must prepare herself, not physically but spiritually; she must be cleansed and properly dressed and, most importantly, she must invite others. She cannot afford to slumber, for the bridegroom may come at any time.

It is easy to fall back to the old self after taking a decision to follow Christ, and to slip into old ways of living. I put it to you that once a proposal has been accepted, the bride never sits and waits passively for the day of the wedding. She gets to work.

She has to find a dress, prepare her body to fit into the dress, arrange the food, find a venue and invite others to the wedding. She knows the value of all this preparation; she will not be embarrassed on the big day. Yet the bride of Christ sits on her laurels and says, 'Here I am, waiting.'

It is during that time of waiting that the enemy tries his best to steal away the bride of Jesus. He tries by all means to make the bride believe that she can manage without her bridegroom. He brings alternative points of view to the bride; the bridegroom is insufficient, not good enough, and he himself is the better option.

She may find herself broke, and the enemy is there with suggestions of ways to make money. Or the bride falls sick, and thinks she must postpone the wedding while she deals with her sickness, perhaps consulting alternative healers, whose source is the enemy. Before you know it, she has become a runaway bride.

The time of preparation separates the real bride from the insincere bride. These are those of whom Paul says, *'They went out from us, but they were not of us'* (1 John 2:19).

The bride of Jesus is not one person, but the whole body of believers. She is portrayed as an individual, but she is all of us – those who claim the name of Jesus and who profess to follow Him. The bride needs to be constantly preparing individually and collectively. Paul says we should not stop fellowshipping together.

As the bride of Christ, we are a single unit, and we stand or fall as the weakest among us stands or falls. When we fall, those who look on will see a stain on the dress of the bride. They will see that instead of 'putting on Christ', as the Bible instructs us to do, we have 'put off Christ'. When the bride is no longer clean and perfumed, she begins to release an offensive smell that marks her as unprepared.

At times, the bride who is waiting runs out of oil for her lamp. Once she walked in the light; now she has run out of oil, and her sister's lamp is no longer sufficient to light her house. She must go and buy her own oil. When all their lamps are full of oil, the virgins bring a bright light into the world. Their light shines so brightly that it attracts the lost, who run towards them. They cannot help the lost unless they are always supplied with oil, and their light does not dim.

Allow this book to make a contribution to your life as a Christian believer, for you form a vital part of the bride of Jesus. May this book empower you in your time of waiting for the groom. Together, let us hold our lamps higher, remain constantly prepared, and use this time so that we are truly ready.

God's Word uses the analogy of the bride and groom to describe the relationship that Christ has with the Church. Jesus is coming soon and He is coming to His bride, *'that He might present her to Himself a glorious church, not having spot or wrinkle or any such thing, but that she should be holy and without blemish'* (Ephesians 5:27).

Jesus is coming for a glorious bride, a beautiful bride without spot or blemish. He is coming to a bride who moves in the power of the Holy Spirit. He is coming to a bride whom He can present to Himself, holy and perfect. He is coming to a bride who has separated herself from the world for Him only. He is not coming for one whose foot is on both sides.

He is not coming to a bride whose lamp is dim, whose temperature is neither hot nor cold; that one, He said He will spew out.

The bride has been washed in the blood and wears a gown that is as white as snow. She has been perfected by the Lord Himself and she is ready for the wedding. She has died to self and risen with Christ. She has put on Christ.

Jesus is coming to a Church that is mature enough for marriage. He is not coming for infants who are not yet ready for marriage. A mature bride is ready to cook, clean and take care of the household, and these days she also goes to work or runs her own business, making a contribution to the family. Jesus wants a bride with whom He will rule the earth.

He is not coming for children who cannot stand up or prepare a home. He is not coming for a bride who does not know her position. He is not coming for one who thinks it is alright to sleep in the neighbour's house occasionally, and who is absent from the home where her bridegroom expects to find her.

The beautiful thing about the story of the ten virgins in Scripture is that they did not quarrel or accuse. The matter was settled; 'go and buy your own'. The Church today fights for the oil, seeking positions instead of positioning ourselves for the coming Lord. It is He who will allocate seats for the bride. Will He find a bickering, splitting Church?

Behold, He comes like a thief in the night. He comes for the bride who is ready and waiting. He comes for the one who is cleansed and exudes a sweet fragrance. He comes for the kingly and priestly bride.

Will you be ready? Will you be glorious? Will Christ shed a tear of joy when He beholds His beautiful bride?

1
The Bridegroom

"And at midnight a cry was heard: 'Behold, the bridegroom is coming; go out to meet him!'

(Matthew 25:6)

Arrayed in royal apparel, highly exalted, perfect in essence and divinity, seated on the right hand of God the Father, is a Man who is God – Jesus Christ. Poets try to devise fitting praises to Him, but adequate words cannot be found. One comes to the point of sitting in adoration, having nothing more to say, just loving the Lord.

It is fitting that the bridegroom is known before we discuss the bride. It is the bridegroom who chooses a wife for Himself. The bride, having received a proposal, considers the prospective husband carefully, seeking to know him in some depth, wishing to know what he offers before she accepts. The people of old lived knowing God the Father, who is invisible, and who revealed Himself to man at various times. To Moses, He spoke in a burning bush, but He was not the bush.

Speaking with God is always a spiritual, supernatural experience, an encounter with God of the universe.

Having seen all that God could do, Israel was quick to turn away and make for themselves a tangible god, a golden calf which they could see and touch. Their neighbours had gods, and Israel sought to conform to the standard of the world. The very thing that God called their forefather Abraham out of – the worship of idols – is what His nation went back to.

Throughout their time in the wilderness, the Israelites were accompanied by the glory of God. He is above all things, and could not be contained in an ark or a tent. He was in the cloud and the pillar of fire, always a little ahead of them, and always a source of comfort. They walked their journey knowing that they could face anything, because Almighty God was with them.

It was fitting that God would later send *'Immanuel ... God with us'*, as Matthew 1:23 describes Jesus. Man has never been at any time without God. Even now, God is with us through the Holy Spirit: *'I will not leave you as orphans, I will come to you ...'* (John 14:18).

The presence of God with man was not sufficient

The Bridegroom

without the full reconciliation of God and Man. Man could walk with God and still be doomed, unless man was reconciled with God. The men who touched the Ark of the Covenant when they thought it was about to fall died because of their assumption; we cannot come close to God unless we are reconciled to Him.

The price for sin had to be paid. The sin that separated man from God in the Garden of Eden had to be paid for, and who better suited to make the payment than He who is perfect and without sin, the Saviour of the world? The Old Testament predicts the coming Saviour, right from the beginning : *'And I will put enmity between you and the woman, between your seed and her Seed; He shall bruise your head, and you shall bruise His heel'* (Genesis 3:15).

The news of the coming Messiah is proclaimed throughout the Old Testament though various types and shadows of the Messiah Himself. There was Moses, calling out the sons of God from Egypt. There was the bronze snake on the pole, which Moses held aloft so that people who looked at it were saved from the venom of live snakes. There was Jonah, who spent three days and nights in the belly of the fish. These events were foreshadowing Jesus.

Jesus is the living expression of God Himself. Phillip, confused about who Jesus was and who the Father was, sought to make a distinction between the two, saying; *'Lord, show us the Father'* (John 14:8). He saw a powerful man before him, one who performed mighty miracles, signs and wonders.

He saw a compassionate teacher who forgave the sins of man. He heard Jesus saying that He came from the Father. He walked with Jesus, touched Him, and talked to Him. Now, he wanted to know the difference between the Son and the Father. Christ replied, *'Have I been with you so long, and yet you have not known Me, Phillip? He who has seen Me has seen the Father, so how can you say, "Show us the Father?" Do you not believe that I am in the Father and the Father in Me?'* (John 14:9–10).

Christ embodies the fullness of God; there is nothing missing. The humanity of Christ did not take away His divinity. He was fully man so that He could identify with humans, be tempted as we are and experience pain as we do; but in all these things He remained without sin. Colossians 2:9–10 says: *'For in Him dwells all the fullness of the Godhead bodily; and you are complete in Him, who is the head of all principality and power.'*

Jesus chose to live as a human being on earth. That did not make Him 'only human'. A mother who walks into a class and becomes a teacher does not cease to be a mother. As a teacher, she holds certain responsibilities and is exposed to a different environment than her home, but she remains a mother, and knows that the

The Bridegroom

classroom is not her home.

Jesus was alive and active in creation. Who better to save humanity than the one who was there when creation was created? *"In the beginning was the Word, and the Word was with God, and the Word was God. He was in the beginning with God. All things were made through Him, and without Him nothing was made that was made"* (John 1:1–3).

It was the will of God to create man, a being who was like Him, formed in His image. This human being, who bore within him the divine imprint, sought to be equal with God. He disobeyed God, having been deceived by the serpent into thinking that God had hidden certain things from him.

Jesus was there in the beginning when man sinned and became separated from God. Jesus came to reconcile human beings with God, to bring us back to the relationship and the fellowship which was lost in the beginning. Only God knows what was broken and only God could fully restore that brokenness. The blood of bulls and sheep was not sufficient to wipe off the filthiness of sin.

Christ upholds all that exists. The earth remains as round as it was when it was created. The rain continues to bring water to the earth and to nourish the plants. The plants continue to grow and beautify the earth. The animals continue multiplying and roaming the earth. Human beings continue to multiply and fill the earth. There has never been a collision of the planets, even though they are all in constant motion. There has never been any confusion between the sun and the moon; neither has one taken the other's place. As long as the earth remains, the seasons come and go. If these things existed as parts of a machine, there would have been a collision long ago. Christ is first in existence, in power and in position. Before the beginning began, the Word was there.

He is the head of the Church and the source of its life. He is the one who started the Church, and the Church belongs to Him. *'... and on this rock, I will build my church, and the gates of Hades shall not prevail against it'* (Matthew 16:18).

The serpent's head was crushed right on the cross, *'Having disarmed principalities and powers, He made a public spectacle of them, triumphing over them in it'* (Colossians 2:15). All the powers of the devil, and all the principalities that exist, were defeated there on the cross.

The bridegroom is the sacrificial Lamb of God. He is the kind of husband every woman would desire; he sacrifices all for us, provides, heals, delivers, leads, guides and eventually died for us. His life, to Him, was less precious than ours, for He laid down His life for us. *'Therefore My Father loves Me, because I lay down My life that I may take it again'* (John 10:17). He owed no one anything. He paid the price for a debt He did not create.

Jesus Himself refers to Himself as the bridegroom. *'Can the friends of the bridegroom mourn as long as the bridegroom is with them?'* (Matthew 9:15). He was responding to someone who asked why the disciples did not fast, as the Pharisees did. In responding the way He did, He introduced the metaphor of the bride and groom, even as He had begun proposing to the people; 'Will you marry Me?' He may not have used those exact words, but the meaning of His life expressed this idea. *'I am the way, the truth and the life, no one comes to the Father except through Me'* (John 14:6).

John the Baptist was glad that He had seen the bridegroom. *'He who has the bride is the bridegroom; but the friend of the bridegroom, who stands and hears him, rejoices greatly because of the bridegroom's voice. Therefore this joy of mine is fulfilled'* (John 3:29). Oh, that your joy and mine may be fulfilled when we hear the voice of the bridegroom. When we hear His voice, like sheep we follow Him.

I don't know about you, but I adore this Man. He is precious. His only thought was to die for us, and He did.

Oh come, Lord Jesus.

2
Chosen

'You did not choose Me, but I chose you and appointed you that you should go and bear fruit, and that your fruit should remain, that whatever you ask the Father in My name He may give you'

(John 15:16).

As a woman I have been approached countless times by men. It is in the nature of men to seek out women. For some it is a joke, for some it is out of lust, and for some, there is a genuine seeking for a partner with whom to spend their life. Walking down the street, a woman is seen and approached by men. An opportunity avails itself whenever, wherever, however, and a seeking man who is bold enough never loses an opportunity.

The love or marriage proposal is done in various ways. Some men have interesting ways of telling their

The Bride of Jesus

beloved how they feel. Some are timid and trip over their tongues just trying to say, 'I love you' and ultimately, 'Will you marry me?' The marriage proposal is a formal occasion, and what you say can make or break that man.

I have always wondered how it makes a man feel when he pours out his heart to a woman and she rejects him. Some men chase after their beloved for years, while for some it is easy. Those who pursue a woman for many years may still end up being rejected and have to settle for someone else.

Of all the women on planet earth, of all the shapes and sizes, the different colours and skin tones, the varieties of beauty (we are all beautiful in the eyes of God), there is just one woman who steals the heart of her husband. He might have shown an interest in other women before, but when he finds the one who surpasses them all in his eyes, he stops chasing. Her 'yes' brings joy to his heart.

Jesus chooses His bride also, as is clear in the scripture above. His disciples, like us, had a tendency of thinking of themselves more highly than they ought. Jesus made sure that they knew the relationship was based not on their choice, but on His. They were accustomed to students choosing the Rabbi they would follow. Not so with Jesus, who instead chose them. How amazing, the thought that we have been chosen by the Lord!

At the same time, we also have to choose and to accept for the relationship to become established. Many die without having an encounter with Christ. Some die having heard about Jesus, but not having an interest. Some walk with believers and acknowledge Christ, but never come to the point of making Him theirs.

Jesus came to His twelve disciples and called them. Peter, Andrew, John and James were fishermen when they were called. Interestingly, two of them had met Jesus earlier; they were with John the Baptist when Jesus came past and John the Baptist said to them, *'Behold the Lamb of God'* (John 1:36). They must have had an interest for they responded positively. *'The two disciples heard him speak, and they followed Jesus'* (John 1:37).

Andrew went to Peter and told him that they had met the Messiah, and Peter in turn followed Jesus. They joined Him and stayed where He stayed, witnessing. They witnessed the early miracles of Jesus, including the water being turned into wine. They got to know Jesus. Jesus had not yet called them – they were interested in Him because of what John the Baptist had said. Having followed Jesus for a little while, these men went back to their fishing business. They were not yet ready. They were not yet called. They were still like many churchgoers whose heart has not yet heard the call of Jesus, 'Come, follow Me.' They were like those who come to church occasionally but do not have a relationship with Jesus.

I have a friend with whom I spent a lot of time with before Christ called me, before I was born again. We were living life, or so we thought. When Christ found me and called me out of darkness into light, I disappeared from her life for a while. My excitement was similar to how the disciples may have felt when they left their father with their boats and servants. It was more exciting for me to follow Jesus and learn about my new-found King than to go to parties.

Sometime later, my friend got sick. I visited and prayed for her many times, and took my pastor to do the same. I told her about Jesus. She needed healing, she was very sick. She heard us and she accepted the prayers. She said all the right words, but did not believe in her heart, and therefore could not confess the Lord Jesus. She later told me that one day, she would accept Jesus and she would be serious about it.

Ironically, that is the same thing I told my husband before I got saved, too. He kept urging me to go to church with him. I would go once in a while and feel that I did not fit in. It did not make any sense to me, because my heart did not believe. I knew about Jesus, for I grew up reading the Bible, hearing about Jesus and God the Father, but Jesus had not yet become real to me.

Christ was not witnessed to in my heart, and I had not come to the point where I understood that *'In the beginning was the Word and the Word was with God and the Word was God'* (John 1:1).

I told my husband that one day, when Christ found me, I would be totally and fully committed to Him. I would not be a visitor who went to church only on Christmas day and Passover.

My friend went through really tough times, but I moved cities and we drifted apart. One day, sick as she was, she called me and told me that she had received Christ; she was saved, born again. Oh, the joy in my heart. It was more than four years since I had left. It had taken that long for her to come to the point where she could *'confess with your mouth the Lord Jesus and believe in your heart that God raised Him from the dead, you will be saved'* (Romans 10:9).

She told me that she was going to church, she was even attending lunch-hour prayer services. Her excitement was audible, and it was clear that she now believed in her heart. She reminded me that she had told me that her time would come.

No matter how much one preaches to a person, this salvation is between Christ and the person. Our role is to prepare the heart for the ultimate proposal; 'follow

The Bride of Jesus

Me.' We preach the Gospel to bring the people of God to the point of hearing, but Christ brings them to the point of believing, then confessing His name.

The fishermen are an example that there are people who follow Christ but have not heard the call to follow. Jesus walked all over Israel, and there was always a commotion, always a crowd. Many heard Him speak and were interested, but their hearts were hardened. Some came and followed because they ate the bread and were filled; they wanted more of the tangible things rather than a relationship with the One who brings the tangible things.

The fishermen had to come to a point of hearing Jesus saying to them, *'Follow me, and I will make you fishers of men'* (Matthew 4:19). That was the ultimate proposal to them, a call with authority. It was not a 'let's go together' kind of call, which presupposes that each knows where he or she is going. Christ called them to a 'come after me, walk behind me, I know the way and you don't, you will get there if you stick with me' kind of a proposal. They did not know much about Jesus, but they accepted His call. It was a marriage proposal, a lifetime-and-beyond kind of relationship. It was not a relationship of convenience, but a covenant kind of relationship.

Many others attempted to follow Jesus, but they were not sold on the idea of a lifetime relationship. They still had issues to deal with. Some had just taken a bride, and were not ready to leave and follow Jesus. Some had too many riches and were not ready to sell everything, give to the poor and trust Jesus for their upkeep. Some still had positions in the synagogue and the temple, and were not prepared to take a chance with a man they did not know much.

They were not sure if this would last. Some came for a little while, and when the teaching became too difficult for them to hear and bear, they walked away.

Imagine a bride who accepts a proposal from a man and then goes back to live with her parents, expecting the bridegroom to just get on with his life. Or a bride who chooses to remain with her riches because she cannot let go, and does not see any riches from the potential husband. Or a bride who wishes to get married but is afraid of what people will say.

These are the people who fill the pews in church; they hear the message but cannot come to a decision. These are the people who want to be buried as if they were believers, although they were just there for social reasons. They fill the forms to become members of the church, but the proposal is not yet accepted.

The Bride of Jesus

They come to church but they do not come to Christ. Theirs is an earthly relationship with the bride of Jesus, not the bridegroom Himself. The friend of the bride is not the bride. The bride becomes one because she has accepted the proposal.

Jesus is calling a bride who will be prepared to leave everything and follow Him. She is the kind of bride who believes that when she seeks after the kingdom of God and His righteousness, all these other things will be added to her life.

She is the kind who believes that Jesus is for keeps. She is the one who is not ashamed of her relationship with the Lord. She is not a Sunday Christian who is different Monday to Saturday. She is not there for convenience, to get something out of the relationship. She is not the kind who sticks around when all is well, and runs away at the first sign of trouble.

The call of Jesus was clear to the disciples, and He continued clarifying the life they were called to through His teaching and preaching. They were to become fishers of men. They were called to a life that was not centred on self. They were called to a life that should bring others into the fold. The bride is called to a marriage in order to multiply. This is not just about children.

It is said that if you give a woman money she will bring groceries, and if you give her groceries she will give you a meal. A woman may walk into the life of a man and find very little, but if she is a good woman she will make sure that there are changes for the good. She makes a home. A good woman builds her house and does not destroy it. So, too, the Church.

The disciples were called into a fellowship that was intended to increase. They were called to bring more to the Kingdom. They accepted the call to work in the Kingdom. Jesus did not promise riches. We know these days that women marry 'blessers' because of money. They bring nothing and they do nothing but milk the husband. Disciples of Christ are not called to take and take, but to receive and give.

The call of Jesus is not conditional upon Him giving us things. He calls believers to come after Him and accept what He gives, sleep where He sleeps, and eat what He eats. A servant is not above his master.

This is a call of a lifetime. Accept it. Open your heart. This is a love proposal. This is a lifetime commitment. This marriage is eternal. This is a call to be the bride of the King of kings, the Lord of lords, and the God of gods. He is no ordinary bridegroom. He is the creator of the bride. He is the key to all things. Life exists and consist in Him. He is 'God with us'.

The Bride of Jesus

The call of God did not start with the disciples in the New Testament. Abraham, for instance, was called by God the Father out of his homeland. He was called out of a people who worshiped idols. God wanted a separation from all that was ungodly and for Abraham to become a father to many nations.

The very nation that ensued from the loins of Abraham is the one whom God called His bride – Israel. He refers to Himself as Israel's husband.

To be the bride to God, Abraham had to leave his family. He did not know the place he was going to but he accepted. God provided and protected him, increased and multiplied his seed until they became a nation, and God took that nation as a wife. This was a type of what was to come through the Lord Jesus. It was a call for these people to be married to this one God, and to belong to Him.

Having established this nation of Israel as His bride, God opened the invitation to the Gentiles too. He calls us all into a relationship with Him, through Christ, reconciling all of humanity to Himself. The type and shadow was meant for us to learn from. We are called to what is eternal – a precious relationship with God.

The best answer to this proposal is, 'Yes, I do. I will follow you.' It is only those who have accepted the bridegroom who can say the words written in Revelation

22:17: '*And the Spirit and the bride say "Come!" and the response of the bridegroom is simply "Surely I am coming quickly"'* (Revelation 22:20).

3
Given by the Father

'I have manifested Your name to the men whom You have given Me out of the world. They were Yours, You gave them to Me, and they have kept Your word'
(John 17:6).

The most beautiful person in the wedding walks in, escorted by her father. He is the one who gives the bride to her husband. He is the one who says, 'The bride price has been paid, here is your wife.'

Although in some cultures there is no bride price, in Africa there is, as there is amongst Jewish families. However, even in cultures that do not have a bride price, the father must still agree to the marriage of his daughter to this man. In some cultures, marriage is even organized by the parents.

The Bride of Jesus

The father will not, under normal circumstances, allow her precious daughter to be married to someone of ill repute who will mistreat her. He wants what is best for his daughter. He wants her to live a good life, to be loved and cherished. He wants her daughter to be married to someone who will take care of her. The love of the father is such that he is protective of his daughter. It is a pleasure and a joy for a father to hand over his daughter in marriage to a good husband.

In the beginning, God created male and female. He then formed the male, a man called Adam. After this, seeing that this man was all alone, God sought a companion for him. He found none amongst the animals. He then made the man fall asleep and took a rib from him as he slept. With the rib, He formed a woman. When this man Adam arose from his sleep, he saw the woman, presented to him by God, and he loved her and called her 'bone of his bones'. That was the beginning of marriage.

It was God who made the woman for the man. He already knew the man, and what he needed. Only God could form a woman perfect for the man, a suitable helper, and a perfect companion. This was a lifetime relationship formed by God Himself.

Soon afterwards, the relationship with God was broken by the man and the woman and humanity continued to grow in a sinful environment. Everyone who

Given by the Father

followed was born into this condition of sin. It is God who initiated the move to bring us back, to reconcile us to Himself. We belonged to Him before, but were separated from Him by our own actions. The relationship between God and man was broken, and only the Creator could mend it.

About the disciples, Jesus prayed, *'I have manifested Your name to the men whom You have given Me out of the world. They were yours, You gave them to Me, and they have kept Your word'* (John 17:6–7). A mission accomplished in unison, the Father and the Son.

It is tempting these days to be influenced by the New Age way of thinking, and focus on Jesus the man while discarding the Father. It is as if the Father's role ended with the Old Testament. It is as if Jesus exists apart from the Father. Many discard the Old Testament as if Christ was not in it. All the while, Jesus says, *'I and My Father are one'* (John 10:30).

It was the Father who gave us to the Son. It was the Father who gave Eve to her husband Adam. It is the Father who released the Son to us so that whoever believes in the Son will have everlasting life. It is the Father who sacrificed His Son Jesus for a sinful people.

It is the Father who has given the Kingdom to the Son and said, *'Sit at My right hand'* (Mark 12:36). You cannot have the Son and not have the Father. You cannot disregard the Father and boast about the Son. They are one and we must expect this oneness to filter down to you and me.

On this earth, the bride normally takes the husband's surname. She is then associated with that family name. She does not take her husband's first name, only the family name. She belongs to her husband but she belongs to the family too, and becomes related to the family. Though she is not married to the father of her husband, she bears his name.

In the Church, the Father of the bride is also the Father of the bridegroom. She is married into the family of the bridegroom and therefore related to the Father. You cannot therefore discard the words of the Father, and elevate only the Son who has been sent by the Father in the first place. What a glorious thing, difficult to fathom; that the God of the whole earth chose to take a wife for His Son, and that she is you and I.

For the Father to select this bride for His Son, he had to know the bride well and see that her qualities are fitting for His Son. This should bring us to our knees; sinful as we were, filthy as we were, the Father saw fit to present us to the Son, not for a temporary washing, but for eternal life. As a wife to my husband, I am grateful to see that my father has a good relationship with my husband. That to me means my father approves. In reality,

Given by the Father

my father did not choose my husband – I did, but he gave his approval. I am also grateful that my father-in-law (he is resting now) accepted and loved me. He was a farmer, and when harvest time came, would always make sure that I received mangos, mealies and peanuts. I would not go there and leave without receiving some gift of his produce. As a daughter-in-law, I belong to the family and am expected to respect and love my father-in-law.

We have a relationship with God that is greater than an earthly one. In the Old Testament, the father is pre-eminent; in the New Testament, the Son is pre-eminent in the gospels, and from the time of the apostles until now, the Holy Spirit has been pre-eminent. Yet in all these things, God is one. The Son is in the Father, the Father in the Son, the Holy Spirit is in both, and we are brought into this triune relationship.

There are 'hangers on' in some relationships. You know those people who hang around a couple but are not related and not true friends. They are there for a while and then move on. In the Church, there are those who come to church for a season and then go back to their normal lives. Some like the idea of church and having someone to bury them, but are not committed to a relationship with the Lord. Such have no intention of seeing the Church succeed.

The Bride of Jesus

Jesus had His fair share of those. His preaching ensured that people were sifted. Those who were not ready, walked away when His teaching did not suit their ideas and lifestyles. It was good when Jesus healed the sick and fed the hungry, but some walked away when He taught them hard truths. Life changing teaching was not acceptable to some, they would have to let go of the things they enjoyed doing which were contrary to the word of God. *'Therefore I have said to you that no one can come to Me unless it has been granted to him by My Father'* (John 6:65).

Since to come to the Son is to come to Father and the Holy Spirit also, we need to know what the Father says, what the Son came to establish and what the Holy Spirit is doing right now.

This is revelation within a relationship. *'I am the way, the truth and the life. No one comes to the Father except through Me'* (John 14:6). Jesus makes it clear that we cannot come to the Father without Him, and likewise, we cannot come to Him without accepting the Father also. We do not get to choose; it is all or nothing. And even though we think we are the ones who make the choice, He, in fact, has chosen us.

4
The bride price is paid

'Knowing that you were not redeemed with corruptible things, like silver or gold, from your aimless conduct received by tradition from your fathers, but with the precious blood of Christ, as of a lamb without blemish and without spot.'

(1 Peter 1:18-19).

Traditionally, in most African countries and in some other cultures, including the Jews, a bride price is paid by the husband to her family before the couple may wed. This is not a purchase as in a commercial transaction, but a seal for the joining of two families. It is not necessarily a God-ordained process, but simply cultural.

The Bible records certain social traditions as well, not putting them forward as law but merely recording them.

The Bride of Jesus

There is, however, something to be learned from this tradition.

I am tempted to work the analogy of the bride price a little here – indulge me! After Adam was created and no suitable companion was found among the animals, God made a woman from Adam's own rib. Such was the sacrifice which Adam was called to make, although he did so without knowing or consenting to it. He arose from his sleep and saw before him 'one like him' and he exclaimed, *'This is now bone of my bones and flesh of my flesh; she shall be called Woman, because she was taken out of Man'* (Genesis 2:23).

Without the rib, there would not have been a woman in the form of Eve. The sacrifice was from his own body. He paid with his rib so the woman could be formed by God. The second Adam, Jesus, gave more than a rib for His bride; He gave His whole life. Man can learn from this – a bride is gained not just by words, but by sacrifice.

Jacob, after running away from his brother Esau, went to stay with his uncle Laban. There he fell in love with his cousin Rachel, and entered into an agreement with her father that he would work for seven years for her hand in marriage. *'Now Jacob loved Rachel; so he said "I will serve you seven years for Rachel your younger daughter"'* (Genesis 29:18).

The bride price is paid

In some communities, it would have been concluded easily; the two would agree to marry and a wedding would be organized – no sacrifice required. Jacob had to work as a shepherd for seven years to earn his bride. After seven years of hard work, when he was ready to marry her, a wedding was organized but he was given the older sister, Leah, instead. He had to work another seven years for Rachel.

That was a high price to pay; fourteen years of work for the woman he loved. Laban became wealthy because of the grace that was upon Jacob; his flocks increased in number, and he did not want Jacob to leave. It was the love that Jacob had for Rachel that made him work such a long time for her. He worked as a shepherd for double the time stipulated – seven years for each woman – yet he loved only one. The bride price is paid out of love, and not obligation.

Interestingly, Jesus is the Good Shepherd who came to lead God's people back to the heart of God. He paid the bride price for us with His own blood.

'For you were bought at a price; therefore glorify God in your body and in your spirit, which are God's' (1 Corinthians 6:20).

Having paid the price for his wives, Jacob had the right to take them to himself. They no longer belonged to

The Bride of Jesus

their father Laban, but to him. They would bear children for Jacob, and he would take them with him when he decided to leave and return to his own home. They were his wives, and he was their husband. The price was paid, and he owed Laban nothing.

Jesus, too, bought us at a price. He redeemed us. Redemption is the action of gaining or regaining possession of something in exchange for payment or clearing a debt. This is exactly what Jesus did.

Here is the bottom line: sin meant death for everyone. Sin was a debt that had to be cleared. A thief goes to court, is found guilty and pays for his debt through jail time or a fine. Until that is paid, he is not free, for he is in debt. If he cannot pay the debt himself, someone may pay it for him and he walks off a free man.

Our freedom was paid for by Jesus with His blood. *'... in whom we have redemption through the blood, the forgiveness of sins'* (Colossians 1:14).

The law until that point provided for the atonement of sins through the blood of animals. The people had to go to the temple at certain appointed times and offer sacrifices so that their sins would be forgiven. This forgiveness was always temporary. When they sinned again they had to come back and sacrifice again.

The bride price is paid

The priest who offered the sacrifices to God on their behalf was also required to offer sacrifices for his own sins. But glory to Jesus, all this has changed.

'But Christ came as High Priest of the good things to come, with the greater and more perfect tabernacle not made with hands, that is, not of this creation. Not with the blood of goats and calves but with His own blood He entered the Most Holy Place once for all, having obtained eternal redemption' (Hebrews 9:11–12).

What manner of husband is this? Enforcing a will and establishing a new covenant even before He marries His bride! *'For where there is a testament, there must also of necessity be the death of the testator. For a testament is in force after men are dead, since it has no power at all while the testator lives'* (Hebrews 9:16

Our earthly husbands have at times to be dragged before lawyers to write a will. Some are so afraid of death, they think that writing a will calls them to an early grave. Some think you might just want to kill them if you know their worth.

But not this bridegroom. He wrote the will even before His bride was born. Before the foundations of the earth were laid, He determined that the price would be paid by Himself. He counted His life less than that of His bride. He willingly died so that His bride could get what

The Bride of Jesus

He had determined she should have – eternal life with God.

'For Christ has not entered the holy places made with hands, which are copies of the true, but into heaven itself, now to appear in the presence of God for us; not that He should offer Himself often, as the high priest enters the Most Holy Place every year with blood of another' (Hebrews 9:24-25).

The people of God are perishing because of a lack of knowledge. The people of God are still sold the idea that they owe someone something for their sins. For some, it comprises going to a booth and confessing one's sins to a priest, who then pronounces forgiveness for the sins. That person has his own sins they have to repent for, and to whom do they go? The tradition was so rigid at times, that people felt condemned if they did not go for confession regularly.

These days, the sick pay a price to be prayed for. The price has already been paid. All those forty lashes on the back of Jesus meant healing for you and me. *'And by His stripes we are healed'* (Isaiah 53:5).

Jesus was stripped, beaten and crucified once and for all for our sicknesses. The price for the bride of Jesus to be healed has been paid. The whips used were made of braided leather, with pottery shards and sharp stones affixed to the ends, which tore open the flesh of the prisoner. With each cruel swing of the whip, blood oozed from His body.

The pain Jesus suffered for us can never be weighed; no prize befits such a punishment. It is one thing for a guilty sinner to be beaten like that. They would have inflicted pain on someone else, and so the punishment might fit the offence. Jesus, His mind focused on us, received that pain willingly because of His love for you and me.

There is a pain that, when inflicted, causes the heart to pound strenuously, although the blow is far from the heart. The normal man being so punished might cry out, 'It was not me, I am not guilty, I did not do it!' Jesus took all that pain in His body without complaint, without sin as He was.

Today, people spit on His face when they make the people of God pay for what Jesus has already paid for. The price is paid – why should we pay again? There is not a single instance in the Bible where Jesus made anyone pay for healing. Even before He was stripped for our healing, no one paid to be healed by Jesus. The disciples of Jesus did not require payment for people to be healed.

People today are paying a lot of money to hear prophecies concerning their lives. What are you paying for? If the word is from God, does the prophet then give God the money? He is the one giving the word, after all – according to their logic, should they not therefore pay God for His word?

Why are you paying the postman for delivering a parcel? As far as I know, the postman is paid by the Post Office, the one who has employed him to deliver the parcel. He is never paid by the recipient of the parcel. Even if it is 'cash on delivery', the money given to the delivery man is taken back to the Post Office. Why then are you paying the delivery man? I ask again!

The delivery man is nothing without the authority, the parcel and the van, given by the Post Office. He has no parcel to deliver unless it is given. Who should be glorified? If a particular delivery man refuses to deliver the parcel, the Post Office will send another one.

Call it what you will – 'planting a seed', or 'giving a love seed' or whatever – it is still payment for healing or prophecy. The woman with the issue of blood had already spent all she had on doctors and whatever help she received from others. Doctors use their brains, skill and knowledge to heal the sick; they deserve payment, for they have studied and worked hard for it.

The gift of God is given to the unqualified, with an instruction to give it freely. No one works for the gift of

The bride price is paid

God. When the woman cured of an issue of blood met Jesus, she brought no seed. She went and took her healing through the hem of His garment. Jesus did not even ask for a camel to travel on when people called Him to come and help them.

When asked by the official, He said, *'I will come and heal him'* (Matthew 8:7). He did not say, 'Pay a deposit before I come.' He did not ask, 'How am I supposed to get there?' He just went.

It is one thing for the Church or a person to decide to bless a servant of God, out of the goodness of their heart, but it is another for a servant of God to ask for payment first from a person in need. There are many grateful people out there who are prepared to plant a seed.

A person plants a seed because they already have a harvest and have put some seed aside to plant for the next year. A seed is planted because the person wants to reap a harvest much later. The decision to plant a seed is taken by the sower.

Now Jesus has already given us healing. He has already released the seed. Your seed cannot make Jesus get new stripes or wounds for your healing.

He has already been wounded. You cannot go to a shop and pay for an item that has already been paid for. If they say 'free', they mean it. Don't pay for it. It is already paid for. If you have money, use it for something else.

There is probably a servant of God who is struggling, and is busy praying to God to assist him financially, and you are not listening to the Lord telling you to go and give that money to the struggling servant. Just because he is not known to be prophetic or to have gifts of healing does not mean he is useless.

Jesus made it very clear, and if the people of God would begin to read the Word of God then they would realise that it is written, *'Heal the sick, cleanse the lepers, raise the dead, cast out demons. Freely you have received, freely give'* (Matthew 10:8).

When Peter and John encountered the lame man at the gate called Beautiful, the issue was not whether or not the man could give them money. The man could not walk or work, so he expected them to give him money, not the other way around. A lame person expected financial assistance from the men who were physically able. I wonder, if Peter had the silver and the gold, would he have given this to the man and then passed on to the temple?

Peter healed the physical disability in the man, consequently, he could go and find work. Today, however, the lame man who cannot work, the sick who have not earned money in months or years, the financially stressed person who cannot meet their basic financial obligations are expected to give money to the physically able person who is not sick, not lame and not incapable of working for his or her money.

It is true that the Gospel has to be funded by the people of God. It is true that the servant of God must be funded to travel and preach the Gospel; each of us is expected to contribute to that anyway. Giving is a principle in the Kingdom.

Adam gave his rib for Eve to be made; the people gave way too much for the building of the tabernacle; the people gave for the temple to be built in Jerusalem, and later they gave for the temple and the walls of Jerusalem to be rebuilt. And in the early Church, the people gave far more that the tithe that people argue about today – they gave all.

'Now the multitude of those who believed were of one heart and one soul; neither did anyone say that any of the things he possessed was his own, but they had all things in common' (Acts 4:32).

The believers gave so that each of them had something to eat. They did not give so that one person was excessively fed, but so that all could have enough. The Church in early Christianity was not centred on one person; the Church was the people, the assembly of believers, and not a four-walled structure which had to be funded by people. Things have changed, of course – there are now structures that people use for assembly, and these must be maintained. That is the responsibility of everyone.

However, the exercise of our gifts for the benefit of one another is free. The gifts of God are freely given so that they may be freely given to others.

Some may use the example of Saul in 1 Samuel 9. When he and his father's servants were seeking the lost donkey, they raised the issue of having something to give to the servant of God, Samuel, who would know where to find the donkeys. That verse of Scripture cannot be used to legitimise payment for prophecy or healing. Why? Because Samuel did not ask for it. Saul was the one who initiated that idea before leaving to see the seer. Moreover, in the whole discussion between Saul and Samuel the prophet, there is not a single instance where money was required.

Elisha refused the payment that Naaman brought when he came to be healed of his leprosy. In fact, the servant of Elisha was struck with leprosy for cunningly taking gifts from Naaman as payment for the healing. If this punishment were to be released on those who behave like the servant of Elisha, there would not be enough space to keep all the leprous servants of God today. Perhaps

The bride price is paid

leprosy is released and we see it not.

Elijah may also be used as an excuse to receive money. He went to a widow and asked for food. There is nothing wrong with a servant of God asking for help when he is in trouble. You cannot be hungry and not state your case. Elijah was fed by ravens which got nothing in return for feeding him after he called for drought in the land (1 Kings 17).

Elijah then found a widow and asked her for water. As she went to get water, Elijah asked for bread as well. He was hungry. The woman did not ask for food from Elijah. Elijah was the hungry one, and he asked, even though the woman had only one more meal. Elijah asked for food and in turn prophetically spoke forth abundance to the woman.

When a hungry person comes to you for food, servant of God, provide that food, no matter who he is. When you need food, ask for food, and bless the person who gives you. When a sick person asks for prayer for healing, pray for them, and they will go before God and thank Him, as well as pray for you. As they pray for God to bless you, blessing will flow. How great it is to receive when we have not demanded!

Do not prey on the desperation of the people of God. Their tears come as a memorial to God. Elisha was given five-star hospitality by a woman who was in need of a son.

She gave freely, expecting nothing in return, but simply recognising the servant of God as a holy man. She was providing a service to a servant of God and asked nothing in return, even though she had a great need – the need for a child.

Elisha asked what she needed, and she responded that she 'lived among her people', i.e. she was content with what she had. It was Elisha's servant who told Elisha that the woman was barren. Elisha, wishing to bless her, pronounced that she would have a child, and it happened. This is the kind of giving and generosity we need today.

The great thing is this: Jesus, in the New Testament, has fulfilled all. He has given us everything. He has freely deposited power within all those who believe. Each one of us is on a journey of discovery in coming to know and use this power. While on that journey, it is our responsibility to overflow with what we have been given, to help others. It is our duty to touch lives. It is our duty to stand against the enemy's attack on the brethren. People are desperate out there. People need the intervention of God. It is not time to take out the calculator and check how much you can make from the number of people in the queue. They are God's people.

The bride price is paid

'But I rejoiced in the Lord greatly that now at last your care for me has flourished again; though you surely did care, but you lacked opportunity. Not that I speak in regard to need, for I have learned in whatever state I am, to be content: ... And my God shall supply all your need according to His riches in glory by Christ Jesus' (Philippians 4:10–11, 19). Now, this was a church that shared what they had with the servant of God. Not out of demand, not out of compulsion, but out of their desire to be a blessing to the man of God.

The bride price has been paid.

The bride owes no one anything.

Her husband has taken care of everything.

Don't you dare make the bride of Jesus pay for what her husband has already paid for!

'People, do not despise a thief if he steals to satisfy himself when he is starving. Yet when he is found, he must restore sevenfold; he may have to give up all the substance of his house' (Proverbs 6:30–31).

5
Follows her husband

'Follow Me, and I will make you fishers of men'
(Matthew 4:19).

The day my husband paid the bride price and we were married, he prepared a feast at home. He had a bride and it was time to celebrate. That meant I had to leave my father's house and come to his house. He could not say he had a wife who was still staying with her father and mother. I packed what belonged to me and went to my husband. The wedding feast ends with the bride going to her husband's home.

This moving house has been practised since time immemorial. When God had finished forming Eve, He presented her to her husband. When Abraham left Ur, he took his wife along.

The Bride of Jesus

When Rebekah agreed to be the bride of Isaac, she was asked if she would go with the men who called her. She agreed and left her family.

The act of following is best presented in the story of Ruth and Naomi. Ruth lived in her husband's home even way past his death. She remained with her mother-in-law, Naomi. When Naomi wanted to return to Bethlehem and suggested that Ruth return to her own place of birth, Ruth revealed the depth of her commitment to the family by refusing to return to her father's house. She understood that she belonged to the family of Naomi. She understood the essence of the covenant of marriage. She said to Naomi:

'Entreat me not to leave you, or to turn back from following after you; for wherever you go, I will go; and wherever you lodge, I will lodge; your people shall be my people, and your God, my God. Where you die, I will die, and there will I be buried. The LORD do so to me, and more also, if anything but death parts you and me' (Ruth 1:16–17).

Ruth went with her mother-in-law back to Bethlehem, a place which Naomi had left during a time of famine. Ruth did not even know Bethlehem, but it was not the place to which she pledged allegiance, it was the family. It was her commitment to be with her husband's family that kept her right behind the old woman. There were no more sons, no wealth, no food nor anything else to entice her to follow Naomi. What kept her there was the relationship that she honoured.

Some marriages break down because of material things. He was wealthy and now is unemployed and poor, so the wife leaves him. Some women leave their husbands because of misunderstandings; he said this and she said that. There is even a neat phrase given to this sort of misunderstanding; 'irreconcilable differences'. I am not trying to downplay the pain that causes some to divorce their spouses. I am just pointing out that some marriages end because of minor issues.

Some men find their wives less attractive after they give birth and are unable to shed the extra weight. They then find someone new with a nice figure who has never borne a child.

The words 'till death do us part' have become meaningless in some marriages. 'In sickness and in health' is null and void to some. I heard of a woman who divorced her husband after a long time of sickness. She could no longer stand him, as he was grumpy and she could not tolerate his moods. She tried for years to support him. Towards the end of his life, she filed for divorce. I am not even judging her for that, I am raising the issue that the divorce was done against a sick person.

The Bride of Jesus

He held on for years when she was around, but gave up after the divorce and passed on.

Some of the fights in marriage are so petty, it is hard to believe that people can't see it. The relationship between God and man was supposed to be eternal. The relationship breaker between God and man was the serpent. The deception was so simple. With, 'Did God say ...?' he planted doubt in the ears of the woman. She entertained him and began believing that there was more to the fruit that God had prohibited them from eating. She wanted more than what God had given her. There were many fruits she could have chosen from, but she wanted the one about which God had said, 'Do not eat.' She was not content with what she had.

God wanted man to live in perfect unity with Him, and to obey Him. Until then, God had related so well with man, communing with him in the cool of the day. They had a solid relationship until the enemy broke the trust. By believing the enemy, the woman broke her trust in God. Then the man disobeyed, and that was it.

To repair this damage, God took the man and woman away from the garden. The relationship was severed, no longer perfect. They still related to one another; God covered their nakedness and provided for them. However, the perfect relationship was broken, and it would require perfect blood to restore and reconcile man to God. It would take a perfect sacrifice to bring man back to where he had once been with God.

Then Jesus!

"Behold the Lamb of God!" The two disciples heard him speak, and they followed Jesus' (John 1:36–37).

The beginning of God's relationship with the disciples was obedience to the call to follow Jesus. They stopped following John the Baptist. He had been a witness; his role was to bear witness to the light, and when the light began to shine the witness was no longer needed. When people began to see the light that was Jesus, they followed Him.

Two men followed Jesus who had not yet been called. One of them, Andrew, went and called his brother Peter. When he had found the light he knew he had to share this news. He would not go to the light alone – his family would come along. They followed Jesus to see where He was staying. Then they went to the wedding feast with Jesus and saw Him turn water into wine (John 2). These disciples then went back to their work, for they were fishermen. They had not yet been called by Jesus, but had followed Him of their own accord, having heard the witness of John the Baptist.

The call of the disciples is recorded in Matthew and Mark, with Jesus later finding Peter and Andrew busy fishing. He went to them and said, *'Follow Me, and I will make you fishers of men'* (Matthew 4:19; Mark 1:17).

The call of Jesus came with authority, very clear and precise. Following is an act of 'going after'. It is not static, it is a moving act. The one who is followed is the one who knows the way and takes the followers to their destination. The follower trusts that the leader knows where he is going. The follower must believe that where they are being taken is where they would want to be.

We would not go to a fire knowing that we will burn simply because someone said, 'Follow me.' There must be evidence of something good in the command, or in the one making the command, for the follower to follow. Even those who are enticed to do bad things, such as commit a crime, do so because they believe some good will come of it for themselves.

Jesus called the disciples to come after Him, not to take a temporary journey. He did not say to them, 'Let's go.' This would have implied that they were equals, who already knew where they wished to go, and were being invited to join someone heading in the same direction. These disciples did not know where Jesus was going; hence the need to follow. It was not a matter of going home first and then following Jesus. Had they done so, they might have lost Him. It was a call to stop what they were doing and go after Jesus.

Follows her husband

Abraham left Ur and went where God was leading him. He did not know this land God had prepared for him. God did not name the place or give him a map. The Bible does not even record the direction in which he set out, whether east or west of Ur. The instruction was simply, 'Leave and go to where I will show you.' This required Abraham to be a good listener to God, and to get up and follow instructions.

God did not ask Abraham if he wanted to leave, or if he wanted to be a father of many nations. God told him to leave and He would make him a father of many nations.

Jesus did not give the men an option by saying, 'Follow me if you want to.' He gave them an instruction which was good for them. Nor did He promise them good things, as God promised Abraham. Jesus told them that they were going to work in the place where they were going, implying a change of profession. They would become fishers of men.

He did not promise that they would be rich after fishing men. Jesus did not promise that they would lack nothing, or that they would not be attacked. He was calling them to work, and the rest was up to Him.

These days people want to follow Jesus not on the terms of 'till death do us part'. They want to follow Jesus

The Bride of Jesus

in order to get a husband, a car, a job, a successful business or physical healing. Their following Jesus is subject to Him giving them what they require. If they don't get it you will hear them saying, 'This thing of salvation is not working for me.' You know then that they did not get what they wanted.

The truth is, salvation does work, for as long as you have Christ, you have everything that matters. You may not have the car, but Christ is eternal. You may not get a husband, but Christ is eternal. You may not even get rich, you may die poor, but Christ is eternal.

Some people, sadly, follow Christ until the point that their prayers are answered. Once the person gets married, then they are too busy for God. The same sister who was 'hot' in church, is now colder than ice. They are now too busy taking care of their husband. They no longer have time for prayer as they need time out with husband. They no longer have time to win souls because they have to cook, clean and go out with their husband. Going to church is now at the bottom of the list. Someone else may love and serve the Lord while they are poor and needy, and when they become rich, get a job or a start a business, they are suddenly too busy for God. They have money to make, not fishes to fish.

Some came forward many times for prayer, were prayed for before they went for that job interview, but

Follows her husband

sadly, they never come back to the place where they found Christ.

Some genuinely come in need of healing. They hear Christ is the solution, their healer. They go for Christ, praying and believing for their healing. Once healed, they feel no pain reminding them to pray, or to fellowship with the brethren. Then church is too far for them. Sadly, Jesus would have to say, *'Were there not ten cleansed? But where are the nine? Were there not any found who returned to give glory to God expect this foreigner?'* (Luke 17:17–18).

Jesus encountered those who wanted to follow 'on condition'. The one could not go because he had taken a wife, and wanted to enjoy marriage instead of going to the feast. The rich young ruler could not follow because he had too many riches. He could not leave his money to follow, for money was more important to him than his spiritual life. There is nothing wrong with being rich, but we are called to a life of wanting Christ only. The rest may follow afterwards, and should never take pre-eminence over Christ.

It is difficult for a rich man to enter the Kingdom, just as a camel cannot go through the eye of a needle. Riches place demands on our time, and even our integrity sometimes. Money has to be taken care of, it has to be secured, and it has to be multiplied. When you trust in your own ability to secure and keep your money, you will not see a need for God once you have your money. Money is a hard task master. It demands our all.

The bride of Jesus is called to follow Him, with or without money, with or without a husband or wife, with or without healing. The bride of Jesus is called to be content in the presence of God. The disciples committed themselves to follow Jesus wherever He went. Their food was the business of Jesus. Even their tax money was the business of Jesus; He sent Peter to get money from a fish to pay their tax.

The disciples followed Jesus and the first thing He did was teach them. It was not a matter of confessing their sins, accepting Jesus as their Lord and Saviour and then going home and continuing with life. No, they had to learn what it meant to be a disciple of Jesus. They had to know how to conduct themselves as the followers of Jesus. The old had to go, and the only way to get rid of it was that they were taught and could recognise the old habits that had to go.

Jesus taught them a new way of life, a new way of thinking. They may have thought being blessed meant being rich, being at peace, and not fighting with anyone. But the first thing Jesus taught them is found in Matthew 5:3–10:

'Blessed are the poor in spirit,

For theirs is the kingdom of heaven.

Blessed are those who mourn,

For they shall be comforted.

Blessed are the meek,

For they shall inherit the earth.

Blessed are those who hunger and thirst for righteousness,

For they shall be filled.

Blessed are the merciful,

For they shall obtain mercy.

Blessed are the pure in heart,

For they shall see God.

Blessed are the peacemakers,

For they shall be called sons of God.

Blessed are those who are persecuted for righteousness' sake, For theirs is the kingdom of heaven.'

This was a very strange teaching, a mindset shift. This was remarkably different from the blessing in Deuteronomy 28. These New Testament blessed ones had no increase in the fruits of their wombs, or their produce, and there was no defeat of their enemies, or a blessing on their store houses. This was a different kind of thinking. You are blessed when you mourn! Why? For it is an opportunity to draw closer to God for your comfort.

A person who has everything and sheds no tear does not need to ask God for anything. Jesus told them, you are blessed when you are a peacemaker. Your blessing is no longer in the battles you win, as it was for David – no, your blessing is now in being peaceful and spreading peace. Your blessing is in your presenting the other cheek when you are slapped. Your blessing is when you say, 'Father, forgive them' and not, 'Let fire come down from heaven and consume them.'

That's a different view of blessing. Jesus came to change the way we think. If the disciples had just believed the words of John – *'Behold the Lamb of God'* – and then went away and omitted the teachings, they would still be calling down fire on their enemies, like Elijah. But a different kind of Elijah was being birthed. The kind that seeks peace, not war. The kind that blesses his enemies instead of cursing them.

They had to sit and listen to how this new kingdom was supposed to unfold, the kind of kingdom citizens they were supposed to be. You may see a baby Christian in church who says, 'I am born again, and don't judge me for keeping my boyfriend, for continuing to get drunk,

Follows her husband

for continuing to dress inappropriately.' That's the kind of a baby who has not yet completed kindergarten classes. They have not been taught that we are to wake up and wash, dress appropriately and go to fellowship. They have not been taught that we don't quit church because someone spoke badly about us.

Jesus remained even when they cursed Him – so what is a little gossip? They have not been taught that when we become born again we become new, we do not go back to our vomit like dogs. They have missed the class that says we do not get yoked with unbelievers; instead you hear them saying, 'I will pray for him to get saved.'

Jesus would not entrust His ministry to people who bunked kindergarten classes. It took Him three and half years to get Peter out of the impulsiveness of reaching for the spear when attacked. He came eventually to the point where he could sit in shackles in jail gladly, and just love the Lord.

One who has been taught can begin to be transformed into the image of Christ. You have to know Christ to become like Him. You have to believe in Jesus to be saved. But to manifest Christ you have to know Him, intimately. You cannot be like that which you do not know.

The Church is filled with servants of God who have never sat down to be taught. They get saved, then

The Bride of Jesus

run and open a church, mess up for a few years, and go around in circles, making the same mistakes over and over again. The stage of sitting down and being taught should not be skipped. Even Paul stayed with the disciples for a while after being saved. This was someone who had been taught the law and knew more than most. After his conversion, he had to sit and listen to the disciples first, then he was fit to preach.

The bride of Jesus has to sit and be taught by Jesus what it means to be His bride, what authority she has in the Kingdom, what responsibilities she has in the Kingdom, and how she is supposed to behave. The responsibility of the bride of Jesus on earth encompasses more than just being a saved people. She is the signpost for the lost people, who need to see Jesus in her and run to Him. She is to be the light of the world, so that people run to the light and get saved. She is to be the salt of the earth, so that people will taste and see that the Lord is good. She cannot be all these if she does not sit down and listen to the instructions of the bridegroom.

When a bride gets married, she is taught by her family how she should behave with her in-laws. When she gets to the family home, she is taught by her in-laws the ways of the family. Despite everything she may have learned in her own family, she has to adapt to the ways of the new family.

Follows her husband

I had to learn a few things when I got married, even the basic things such as the food that my husband loves. In my own home, our staple food, pap, was cooked differently from the way my husband liked it. His family keeps the mealie meal in water for a few days until it becomes sour, then it is boiled and a little fresh mealie meal is added later. I was used to cooking braai pap, which is what we ate at home. It took me some time to learn this new way. I tried cooking braai pap for my husband and he complained until I learned to cook his pap. Now I am used to that kind of pap, and it is second nature to cook it.

One of the other things I had to learn from my husband concerned the source of our fights – cultural differences. I grew up in a family where I call my brother by his name; he was taught to call his older brother 'Brother So-and-so'. To his mother, calling one's older sibling by name is disrespectful. Even when the age difference is very small, they still call each other respectfully in that way. We had a lot of fights because I did not understand why he made a big fuss over something that seemed immaterial to me. It may have been a minor thing to me, but to him it was a cultural foundation.

The disciples followed Jesus and were taught how to live a life that pleased God. As they followed Christ, they observed what He was doing. Observing is defined as looking at a thing and recording it as significant. So they watched Him do things and recorded His actions and manner as significant.

As Jesus went about, He found demon-possessed men. These men had been in their village for a long time, and no one knew what to do with them. They were a nuisance, and people were scared of them, avoiding the tombs where the men lived for fear of being pelted with stones. The demons recognised Jesus from afar. This was something new to them, and they cried out to Him, begging Him to send them into the pigs, which He did. The demon-possessed men were freed. The people came and witnessed this miracle, then asked Jesus to leave. It was too much for them; the whole herd of pigs had gone into the water and drowned. What more might this man do? He had to go.

The group went to Peter's house, where they found his mother-in-law sick with a fever. It was nothing serious, really. It may have been the kind of flu where we take to our beds for a day, then arise feeling rested and ready to go on. We have all sorts of home remedies for small ailments like flu. Yet for Jesus, the fever required a healing response, not sleep. He lifted her up and immediately she was well enough to wait on them. There is no minor or major sickness with Jesus, the disciples learned.

Follows her husband

They would later see Jesus healing the woman with the issue of blood without His being involved; He did not even know about it, engage with the woman or even touch her. She came from behind and touched the hem of His garment. She did not ask for permission, she did not ask for prayer. She did not touch His person, His flesh. His garment was a source of healing for the woman. The disciples learned that healing could come through things also, when those things were connected with the source of power, Jesus.

They also saw Him healing a man who had been sick for 38 years. He had lost all hope of healing. He had been waiting by the pool of Bethesda to receive healing each time the angel stirred up the waters, but could never get to the water in time when this happened.

Jesus approached the man, and asked him if he wanted to be made well.

In many instances, people came to Jesus to ask for help. This time, they observed that Jesus was moved with compassion, without the man having to ask for help. Jesus told the man to stand, take up his mat and go home. The same man who could not walk to the pool arose and walked by himself. He was not helped up like Peter's mother-in-law. By a word, this man was healed.

The Bride of Jesus

When Lazarus got sick and Jesus was told, he did not rush to heal him. He let him die and then told His disciples that He would go and raise him up. A man who had been dead for four days would start to decay, as they did not have mortuaries then. Jesus went to the tomb and called out a dead man. He did not touch him to make him alive. The Word of God came to the ears of the dead man and those ears responded to the voice of God. The dead man came alive and left the tomb.

The disciples observed Jesus healing a woman who was afflicted by a spirit of infirmity and could not raise herself up. She walked bent down. She was in the temple and it was the Sabbath day. Jesus healed the woman on this very day, when work was not supposed to be done. 'My Father is always working,' said Jesus, and He followed His Father in order to do good. A human being was more important to Him than being able to tick a righteousness box. Time was not of the essence when it came to healing.

Jesus went on to open the eyes of a blind man. For one man, Jesus even spat on the ground and made mud with His saliva, then applied this to the eyes of the man. He told him to go wash in the pool of Siloam, and after the man did so, he could see. He had been blind all his life. He was born like that, for God had made him that way, and then God changed his situation.

Follows her husband

Today we tend to think that the way we were born is what God wants for us permanently. You may seem as if you don't accept God's creation when you seek healing for a disability you were born with. His disciples saw Jesus heal His own creation. He made the man blind, and He was able to make him see. Those who were lame, deaf, and mute were also healed. There was no excuse for remaining in a disabling situation when Jesus was around.

Having observed Jesus for such a long time, the followers of Jesus eventually had to do what He did. *'Most assuredly I say to you, he who believes in Me, the works that I do he will do also; and greater works than these he will do, because I go to My Father'* (John 14:12). A student goes through a learning process and must eventually master the lessons and be able to do them.

The disciples went out after Jesus sent them, and came back excited, reporting that even demons submitted to them. When Jesus left for heaven, the disciples were faced with a test of their faith. All that they had learned was now to be done by them, but without His physical presence. He was no longer there to rescue them, as He had been when they were unable to cast out a demon from the epileptic boy.

The real test came after the infilling that happened on the Day of Pentecost, right there at the gate called Beautiful. What better place than the busy temple gate, where the religious people were going in and out. Some were probably gloating about how they had got rid of the controversial Rabbi who had wreaked havoc in the temple and had led multitudes away from their control.

A man sitting by the gate, lame from birth, looked up at Peter and John. He was expecting alms from them. They had a choice. If they had money, they could have given it to him and moved on. It would be counted as kindness shown to a beggar. But these two disciples had observed the Lord doing miracles to such people. They could not just pass with the words, 'I don't have silver or gold.' Peter looked intently at him and said, *'Silver and gold I do not have, but what I do have I give you: In the name of Jesus Christ of Nazareth, rise up and walk'* (Acts 3:6).

The man arose, leaping, and walked into the temple, praising God. He had a testimony. This Jesus who was dead, though some said alive, had healed him only by a word spoken by the disciples. Peter had the boldness to do this miracle because he had followed Jesus closely and saw Him do it.

The Church today could achieve much more if the works of Jesus were observed. Jesus is the same today as He was all those years ago, and is still healing people. The question is, have people observed what He did and do they believe they can do it all too – or are they content with dressing up and going to church on Sundays? Oppressed people go in and out of church every Sunday and no one is bothered to cast demons out which oppress them.

The Church today has seen a rise in false prophets and pastors. They perform miracles and people run to them. People are not prepared to sit and observe the work of Jesus. People are not prepared to sit and be taught first so that they can identify a false prophet from far. Those who acknowledge the false prophets reject the true prophets, and say boldly, 'We don't believe in prophets.' How can the bride of Jesus have victory if she is not prepared to sit and be taught and observe what Jesus is doing?

When you have followed Jesus to the letter, you will be like the true disciples of whom it was written: *'These who have turned the world upside down have come here too'* (Acts 17:6).

6
Intimate

'But it is good for me to draw near to God; I have put my trust in the Lord GOD, that I may declare all Your works' (Psalm 73:28).

Deep dreams and fears are revealed during a time of intimacy, a time of openness or nakedness before another. I am not even talking adult matters here. Girls may sit over a cup of tea and pour their hearts out to one another. Boys sit around a braai stand and talk about issues. Couples close the door behind them and cuddle up and whisper to one another. Intimate moments like these are precious.

Intimacy brings a couple closer, building a strong bond of love for each other. Intimacy is what makes a husband rush home from work, so that he may hold and touch his wife. She, too, wants just to fall into his strong arms. Loving couples spend hours sitting and talking about nothing, laughing over silly jokes.

At such times plans are made. Buildings are started in such moments; this one wants a bigger bedroom, the other wants a study, another may want an extra garage, and so forth. At times like these, the one who has suddenly become broody states her case. It is at such times that even the things that have hurt the other person come to light. 'I did not like what you did,' he or she might say, knowing that the words will not be rejected, but considered. These are the sane conversations we have because the setting is right.

There are some things that can be tolerated in people when they are far from us. Bad habits can be overlooked when you don't live with a person. When you get close to someone, however, you get to know them, and their little ways may grate at first. Later you come to understand why they do the things they do.

In the intimate moments, you get to understand the other person deeply and eventually to accept them with all their flaws. You become comfortable with nakedness before the person you love. You drop your fears, share your deep thoughts and secrets. You share the things you would not want anyone else to know about you. There should never be any barriers in an intimate relationship.

Intimate

The Bible tells us of a woman, who is known only as a 'sinful woman', already an outcast in the society she lived in, who performed an act that came from the depths of her heart, and she came out a better person. Jesus went to eat at the house of a Pharisee, and as they were eating, this sinful woman approached Him, opened an alabaster flask with fragrant oil, and washed the feet of Jesus. She then dried them with her hair and anointed His feet with the oil (Luke 7:36–39).

This woman came heavily burdened, as she had lived her life as a sinner. To the religious people she was probably headed for eternal damnation. She, on the other hand, sought an opportunity to present herself to the Lord. She had decided to fall at the feet of God rather than man.

This was her act of intimacy, and as she washed His feet with her tears, she may have been pouring out her anguish. She did not say a word. She did not recite, 'Forgive me Lord, for I am a sinner.' She came close enough to the Lord to show her remorse. She showed reverence to the Lord. As filthy as she was in the eyes of man, she placed herself at the mercy of God.

In that short intimate moment with the Lord, she received what all those self-righteous people did not receive. *'Your sins are forgiven'* (Luke 7:48).

The Bride of Jesus

A husband and wife need such times of intimacy, which go beyond physical interaction. They need a time of getting to know each other; their fears, dreams, shortcomings, desires and failures. God desires us to get that close to Him, close enough to pour out our hearts to Him. Close enough to be naked before Him. Not that He does not already know everything about us, but He would rather we present ourselves to Him. None of those reclining at the table, sinners as they were, received the forgiveness of Jesus as the woman did. Jesus knew all their sins.

In fact, the Pharisee had not even shown the Lord real hospitality. Intimacy allows one to speak out the painful or embarrassing things, knowing that you will not be judged.

When Adam and Eve were in the Garden of Eden, they were not conscious of their nakedness. They walked freely without care, without shame. When God came to see them, they enjoyed a time of conversing with their Creator, free of limitations or fear. God knew them and they knew God. Sin opened their eyes so that they saw their nakedness. Their nakedness became an issue to them only after they sinned, not before. Guilt kept telling them they had fallen short and needed to cover up. Man has been covering up his sins ever since.

Intimate

Unless a thing is uncovered, it cannot be cleaned up, cannot be improved or changed. The enemy wants to keep the people of God away from Him, and have them think God can do nothing for them. When Judas realised his mistake, he did not rush to say sorry to Jesus. Instead, he went away and hanged himself.

Satan will use you and cause you to commit sin, and when he is done with you, he will stand on the other side and point a finger of accusation. You will feel you cannot go to God. Yet the one thing man needs in sticky situations is God.

Another who uncovered his sins before God was Zacchaeus. A man of short stature, challenged by the towering figures of everyone in the street and pushed by his desire to see the Lord, he climbed a tree. That got him noticed, and Jesus called him to come down, then went to dine at his house. At dinner time, Zacchaeus, without being asked or told his misdemeanor, cleared his conscience: *'Look, Lord, I give half of my goods to the poor; and if I have taken anything from anyone by false accusation, I restore fourfold'* (Luke 19:8).

Indeed, salvation had come to his house. He had come clean without any prompting. The truth was not forced out of him. It was his close encounter with the Lord that enabled him to see his mistakes and to make amends. Intimacy is not only about the admission of sins.

The Bride of Jesus

It is also a time of getting to know the heart of the person you are close to.

The gospel according to John is such an intimate book, and I am drawn to it more than the other three gospels. I get to know the heart of the Lord by reading that book. Compared to Matthew who tends towards legalism, traditionalism and cultural bias, John captures more of Jesus' heart, recalling what He said rather than what He did. Through John, we get to know the 'why' of Jesus:

'For God so loved the world that He gave His only begotten Son, that whoever believes in Him should not perish but have everlasting life' (John 3:16).

Why did Jesus come, why did He die? Because God loved the world. We get to know the extent of the love of God towards us. We are introduced to the Gospel as not about avoiding hell but receiving the love of God. We get to know God who is loving and not holding a judge's gavel, pronouncing judgment upon sinners.

This gospel reveals who Jesus is. There are more 'I am' statements by Jesus in the book of John than the other gospels:

'I am the bread of life' (John 6:35).

'I am the light of the world' (John 8:12).

'I am the door of the sheep' (John 10:7).

'I am the good shepherd' (John 10:11).

'I am the resurrection and the life' (John 11:25).

'I am the way, the truth, and the life' (John 14:6).

'I am the true vine' (John 15:1).

'Most assuredly, I say to you, before Abraham was, I AM' (John 8:58).

John recorded for us who Jesus is. He was close enough to the Lord to hear His heartbeat. *'Now there was leaning on Jesus' bosom one of His disciples, whom Jesus loved'* (John 13:23). He was not just a disciple, he was not just following – he was receiving the love of the Lord.

None of the other disciples viewed themselves as especially loved by the Lord. Surely, Jesus loved them all. But John expressed this because he felt it, it mattered to him. His closeness to Jesus was to the point where the others asked him to ask things of the Lord. Anyone could have asked Jesus anything. They were all reclining at one table, so distance was not an issue.

When there is a tough matter to be dealt with, the closeness of the relationship makes it easier to deal with it. It was easier for John to ask certain questions, not because he was a favourite, but because somehow He knew he was loved. He was not afraid to ask intrusive or difficult questions of the Lord.

The Bride of Jesus

The rest of them did not have the confidence to ask certain questions, not even Peter. The question at the Last Supper was who would betray Him. How could anyone betray Jesus? Of all of them, the one whom Jesus loved would be bold enough to ask.

I have a very close relationship with my father. I am daddy's girl through and through. I love my mother, too. Growing up, if the rest of my siblings wanted something, they would ask me to ask Papa for it. He could not say no to me. I was not spoilt, though. I was level headed and discussed serious issues with Papa. Our closeness made it easy for me to converse with him.

Now that I am grown up, if Mama wants something, she sends Papa to ask. No matter how broke I am, I will send the money asked. He is not demanding, and he only asks when there is a need. I love my parents and I am loved by them.

The relationship between the bride and the bridegroom, the Church and Jesus, ought to be intimate. Each one of us ought to see ourselves as the disciple whom Jesus loves. Once you reach that point, you can talk to the Lord about anything.

Jesus wants to hear what you desire, what you are afraid of, what you have done or failed to do, where you want to go. Jesus also wants to share His plans for you,

Intimate

His desire for your life, His desire for the Church. It is when you sit down and dine with the Lord that you get to hear Him speak. Not in the wind, not in the earthquake, but in the whisper.

We get busy these days. We are up and running, going to work, doing business, studying. We don't have the time, like the families we see on television, who sit and eat breakfast together, and talk about things early in the morning.

We are already late. The husband is already hooting and the wife is putting the second layer of foundation on her face. If Jesus were to walk through the wall like He did with the disciples, we might not even recognise Him. We might just say, 'Hold up, Jesus, I'll speak to you later.'

Jesus wants to converse with us. He wants to impart His guidance in an atmosphere of love. When you ask people why they do what they are doing for the Lord, some will say, 'I had a desire or a conviction.' What did the Lord say about it? 'I did not ask the Lord. People prophesied this and that over my life.' The question is, what did the Lord say about it?

Receiving instructions from the Lord is not as easy as a child receiving instructions to fetch a parent's glasses. Jesus requires you to sit down and listen, ask and

The Bride of Jesus

listen some more. We want to do mighty things, like the great servants of God in the past, yet we are too busy to give the Lord the time to unfold His plan. How can He trust us with great assignments when we cannot sit and listen to His plans? We want to bring half-cooked ideas to Him to rubberstamp.

You want to get married, but you don't ask the Lord about it. You bring a guy or a girl once your heart is made up and say, 'Lord here he is, he is nice, funny, has a good job, loves his family, is kind and giving ...' Is he saved? 'He is a good man, he will change, you will see, you will save him, I will pray about it.' When God is not in it, down it goes to His permissible will, not His perfect will.

'Where can I go from Your Spirit? Or where can I flee from Your presence?' (Psalm 139:7). He is everywhere. He is close enough to whisper to you – He just seeks your attention.

There is a song by Michael W Smith, *Draw me close to you;* an inspirational plea for a close relationship with the Lord, this is what God desires from a believer.

God does not force anyone, but wants His children to come close to Him. David had times of seclusion, times of betrayal, and times of war, and in all these times, he reached out to God. When fear set in, he poured out his heart to God. In the wilderness where there was no one to listen, God was there. Even when he walked through the valley of the shadow of death, he feared no evil because God was with him. What do you do when you go through your valley? Call a pastor? Or call God?

'O God, You are my God; early will I seek You; my soul thirsts for You; my flesh longs for You in a dry and thirsty land where there is no water. So I have looked for You in the sanctuary, to see Your power and Your glory' (Psalm 63:1–2).

In the midst of his difficulties, the road became bearable for David. He was strengthened many a time, failed many a time, and rose up again. He cried to the Lord and He answered him. He knew and felt the love of God. Even when he failed, he ran to God and poured out his heart. Oh, that you would also run to God and not away from God.

'Call to Me, and I will answer you, and show you great and mighty things, which you do not know.' (Jeremiah 33:3).

The answer you seek may not be in the prophet you admire so much, it may not even be in your pastor. It is in hearing the Word of God. People are running around paying money to get 'thus sayeth the Lord'. The time and money taken to get to the point of being told your house is blue, your car is red, your stand number is 476 – that time could be used to hear what the Lord says to you. In the end, you are told what God says in the Word. I am not in any way looking down on prophets; God has given the gift of prophecy for the Church to benefit. Yet God has not taken away the relationship between Himself and His people. There is only one mediator between God and man. The rest of us are signposts to show you the direction. You must journey by yourself to the wedding feast.

We cannot run with just the words told to us by others. The effect will not last. We need the Word of God, for this is what sustains us when we face challenges. Some servants do not have a memory of a time when God called them; they only know that 'someone' told them about their calling. Even if He speaks softly, let Him speak, and listen well. We might miss the first call for lack of intimacy with the Lord, or from being dull of hearing.

All of us, even if we are informed of our calling by others, need to go to the Lord for confirmation. We may need to wrestle with God, just like Jacob did. Hearing His call is not always straightforward or easy.

I have a prophetess friend, dear to my heart. She knew her calling before I did. The prophetic gift can be intimidating, I must say. All of a sudden here is someone who says, 'I hear this,' 'I see this.' Being close to her was something others desired. But it brought me no special

Intimate

benefits in the department of 'thus sayeth the Lord'. She would not budge. She would rather we go to the threshing floor than have me ask her what God was saying. She would not speak on demand, but spoke at the inspiration of the Lord. Many times Prophetess Mphata has said to me, 'Ask your Father,' even in my desperate times. I thank God for sending a servant like her.

When God decided to reveal my calling, I behaved like Samuel at the first call. I asked, 'Did you call me?' I got no answer. Then I went to Mphata. Her answer was 'ask your Father'. She dismissed me. That was 27 October 2011. I went back and asked my Father and did not hear a thing. I went on with life. In October 2012, I had a two-week battle with the Lord.

I held on for dear life like Jacob, saying, 'I will not let you go until you bless me.' I did not tell my friend, lest she dismiss me again, but battled in prayer. I got desperate. I pleaded, begged, made promises, tried to bribe and did all I could.

I slept begging and woke up begging: 'Lord I know you are here and you are saying something, my ears are dull to your hearing. Open them to hear!'

On the morning of 27 October 2012, at the close of this battle and without sharing any of it with my friend, I said to God, from my heart, 'Whatever you say, I will do it, Lord.' Then God used the very same friend to confirm my calling. She did not even know of my question, she just obeyed and sent me a message – three words: 'Apostle Carol Nkambule.' I did not reply to her, as I was in conversation with the Lord. She was being her crazy, prophetic self. 'God', I said, 'not that one, it's too big, too controversial, I am a woman, what would people say'. And so on I went, like Moses. While I was on my knees, God reminded me of all the promises and the bargaining I had done. I accepted my calling. My friend still did not know.

That night, the Lord revealed three things to me through a dream. They were distinct, yet concealed. I needed interpretation and over the next week, I received it. The first was my role in the body of Christ, revealed through a symbol in the dream – an anchor.

The second was the unction to function in a particular role, revealed through my prophetess friend. In the dream, I saw the number 211. When I told my friend about this, she immediately said, 'Let's open Scripture.' There it was, Revelation 2:11: *'He who has an ear, let him hear what the Spirit says to the churches.'* The third symbol was books; the same night, I received the first message, which has now birthed this book, and I have been writing and publishing ever since.

It took three events over three years for my calling

Intimate

to become clear to me. The first was a call in 2011, then nothing happened for a full year; a year later the Lord took me through two weeks of wrestling with Him, followed by a week of revelation and confirmation. Blessing and release came in 2013, and I have been living, by His grace, in that calling ever since.

All of the significant steps in this journey took place on 27 October. During this period, none of the people who played a role were requested to pray for me and tell me what the Lord had said. God used them, however, to confirm His words to me. I only explained to them later what was happening. It was a glorious and humbling experience. He is indeed a rewarder of those who diligently seek Him. You cannot be a bride who does not have intimacy with her husband and expect the relationship to last. If you are not intimate with each other, who are you intimate with?

He wants to converse with you, as he did with Adam in the cool of the day. Seek, and you will find.

Knock, and the door will be opened to you.

7
Pursues holiness

'And you, who once were alienated and enemies in your mind by wicked works, yet now He has reconciled in the body of His flesh through death, to present you holy, and blameless, and above reproach in His sight' (Colossians 1:21–22).

The beauty of being married to someone is the expectation and the meaning of the word commitment; he or she is yours exclusively. It is a good feeling to know that there is one person in the whole world who has agreed to be yours only.

It was a joy to me to hear my husband asking me to be his wife. He had many choices. There were skinny ones, light-skinned ones, more beautiful ones; there were famous ones, there were rich ones, there were holy ones – but he chose me. The mystery of marriage is that there

The Bride of Jesus

is no valid reason why he chose me, except that he chose me. It can't be beauty, for there are many more beautiful, and it can't be intelligence, for there are brighter ones. I was sufficient for him as I was. Of course, there are good things about me, too, that made him choose the way he did – all I am saying is that there will always be a case for a different choice, but he did not change his decision.

He set me apart from all that was available and made me his, and similarly, he set himself apart for me. I can look at him and say, 'He is my husband' – not 'ours'.

The first man had an exclusive relationship with one God. Man belonged to God, and was the only being created in the image of God. It was a relationship that should have endured forever. The sin of man was in submitting to the instructions of the serpent instead of remaining in submission to God. The man and the woman no longer belonged exclusively to God. The serpent had been made their master, telling them what to do. Adam belonged to Eve alone until they died. Adam said of the woman, *'This is now bone of my bones and flesh of my flesh'* (Genesis 2:23). There was no sharing her with anyone. Polygamy came afterwards, and was never the plan of God.

The word 'holy' means being separated for God, dedicated or devoted to the service of God; it describes something that is sacred, exalted or worthy of complete devotion; something that is perfect in goodness and righteousness, having a divine quality.

The Hebrew word for holy is *qodesh* meaning 'apartness, set-apartness, separateness, sacredness'. Holiness is not primarily about being sinless. Holiness depicts something or someone as belonging exclusively to God, separated for Him, devoted to Him, sacred for Him. It is being somewhat like the section on forms which says 'for office use only'. God Himself is holy, separate and above all else. He is one of a kind.

God desired to have a people who looked like Him, who belonged to Him, who looked up to Him and who were devoted to Him. He had that in Adam until he sinned. Throughout the Old Testament, we see men and women whom God used for His mission and purpose. They had to be separated from worldly people, however. God's people must belong to Him and Him only. *'You shall have no other gods before Me'* (Exodus 20:3).

God required of Abraham to come out of idol worshipping Ur in order to release his blessing. Abraham had to be separated from his family, friends and community. God required Israel to come out of Egypt, and to go to a place where they worshipped Him only. In the wilderness, when the people turned away from serving God and made a golden calf, they were punished.

The Bride of Jesus

It is amazing that the same people who said, 'All that God has said, we shall do' broke the very first commandment and made a god for themselves.

Like Israel, we are called to an exclusive relationship with God. He is not to be compared to others, He is not to be replaced with others, and He is not to be assisted by other gods.

I was in India once, and our driver had little gods in his car. I asked him why he had so many gods and how he prays to them all. He said he asks the first one, and if he does not get his answer, he asks the next god, and so on. I said to him, 'So you always have a plan B.' He said 'yes', and we laughed about it. In essence, there was always a possibility of failure with his gods, so he would have to move to another. I don't know how he attributed answered prayer to one of the gods – how would he know which god had answered him?

Our God is incomparable, irreplaceable, unparalleled and unmatched.

Holiness is living a life that is separated for God – doing the thing God wants us to do and leaving the things that are not pleasing to Him. A tea cup is meant to be used for tea and not for carrying sand. It is set apart for a specific use. We, too, should be set apart to be used by God.

Pursues Holiness

He Himself is separate and sacred, untouched by idols or other 'gods', and He expects us to be the same.

'Therefore put to death your members which are on the earth: fornication, uncleanness, passion, evil desire, and covetousness, which is idolatry ... But now you yourselves are to put off all these: anger, wrath, malice, blasphemy, filthy language out of your mouth ... Therefore, as the elect of God, holy and beloved, put on tender mercies, kindness, humility, meekness, longsuffering; bearing with one another, and forgiving one another, if anyone has a complaint against another; even as Christ forgave you, so you also must do' (Colossians 3:5; 8; 12–13).

We are called to a life that separates us from things like fornication, idolatry, anger, etc. We ought to be like God. He is merciful and kind, and we ought to be likewise.

'Be holy for I am holy' (1 Peter 1:16).

This is a simple instruction. God wants us to be like Him. We ought to be separated from sin, devoted to Him and available for Him. God does not expect us to be what He is not. When the world's standards change, we are called to remain as required in the Bible. *'For your Maker is your husband, The LORD of hosts is His name; and your Redeemer is the Holy One of Israel; He is called the God of the whole earth'* (Isaiah 54:5).

This is the relationship that was established with a covenant between God and Abraham: *'And I will establish My covenant between Me and you and your descendants after you in their generations, for an everlasting covenant, to be God to you and your descendants after you'* (Genesis 17:7).

This covenant was sealed with blood. The circumcision of every male child was a sign of that covenant. The children of Abraham belonged to God because of it.

This relationship has held from the time of Abraham until now. When the Israelites dwelt as foreigners in Egypt, God called them out from among the Egyptians. They were His people and Egypt had no right to keep them. He wanted His own.

'I will take you as My people, and I will be your God. Then you shall know that I am the LORD your God who brings you out from under the burdens of the Egyptians' (Exodus 6:7).

The biggest charge God had against Israel was adultery. Even after the establishment of the covenant, Israel broke faith so many times, committing adultery with other gods made of stones and trees. God used very strong words for the Israelites in such cases; He called them harlots. It was a great offence to God.

Pursues Holiness

How can those who are created choose to worship fellow created things instead of the Creator?

'Then I saw that for all the causes for which backsliding Israel had committed adultery, I had put her away and given her a certificate of divorce; yet her treacherous sister Judah did not fear, but went and played the harlot also. So it came to pass, through her casual harlotry, that she defiled the land and committed adultery with stones and trees' (Jeremiah 3:8–9).

Israel made gods of created objects, and worshipped other gods. It is adultery to have a husband and run after others. God is a jealous God. He will not share His glory with another, for no other god deserves the glory. All the materials used to make the other gods were made by God. He created the tree that is cut and shaped into a figure, as He created the stone and the gold. Dagon could not stand alongside God, who created the very substance that was used to fashion the image of Dagon.

'How shall I pardon you for this? Your children have forsaken Me and sworn by those that are not gods. When I had fed them to the full, then they committed adultery and assembled themselves by troops in the harlots' houses' (Jeremiah 5:7).

In the house of the Lord today, churches have made crosses with the image of a man on it, and they bow before it. Whether they are praying to it or not, they are bowing to an image that represents Jesus. Even worse is when they begin to bow to the man of God instead of the God of man.

'You erected your shrine at the head of every road, and built your high place in every street. Yet you were not like a harlot, because you scorned payment. You are an adulterous wife, who takes strangers instead of her husband' (Ezekiel 16:31–32).

To a married couple, adultery is a deal breaker. A lot of divorces are caused by adultery. Adultery makes the one who is cheated question their sufficiency. 'Am I not beautiful enough? Am I not smart enough? Am I not satisfying him? What is wrong with me?' If a man is satisfied with his spouse, why does he need to find another person and commit adultery with her?

God divorced Israel many a times because of adultery. His divorce always brought harm to the people. They lost the protection of God and became vulnerable to their enemies. Read the book of Judges to realise the extent of Israel's harlotry and its consequences for the people of God.

The Word of God points us to Jesus. He is the way, the truth and the life. No one comes to the Father except through Jesus. *'Jesus said to him, "I am the way, the tru-*

th, and the life. No one comes to the Father except through Me'" (John 14:6).

The way to the Father is now through the Son – not through the law, not through self-righteousness, but through the Son. It is no longer the blood of bulls that brings forgiveness, but the Son of God. The price has been paid for the sins of many. He who knew no sin became sin for us.

Jesus expects us to be holy unto God, to be set apart for Him. You cannot have Jesus and serve money. You cannot have Jesus and consult a medium. You cannot have Jesus and worship a human being. Lifting a human being to the place of God is idolatry. People think that since they are not worshipping graven images, they are free of idolatry, yet they have made man an idol.

You don't have to bow down and pray to a man to be an idolater; simply to depend on man instead of God, to trust man for your solutions rather than God, to praise man for your breakthroughs, is to make of man an idol. You have put aside God and made this man your way-maker. People today are ready to defend and kill for a 'man of God'. They have moved from the God of man to the man of God.

People have replaced God with tangible things. They look at a bottle of water as the solution, sans God.

The Bride of Jesus

Remove the bottle of water, and they feel bereft. They trust in a bottle of oil instead of God. Remove that bottle of oil and they will not sleep – they have to replace it. They cannot just close their eyes and pray to God who sees us no matter where we are. People put a sticker or a photo of a human being in their cars and believe they are protected by that person. The same person has bodyguards securing him, but his picture is supposedly a shield for the followers.

People have moved from *'The God of my strength, in whom I will trust; my shield and the horn of my salvation, my stronghold and my refuge; my Saviour, You save me from violence'* (2 Samuel 22:2). Instead they say, 'This sticker will shield me from witches. Demons will see the photo of my prophet and run away.'

The Word of God provides for our healing. Some people have come to a point where they believe that the water itself has the healing power, rather than God. While the water may have been prayed for, God can heal with or without water. Remove the water, and the person is convinced he has nothing and healing will not occur. Remove the oil, and the person is distraught. People have moved from *'For I am* the LORD *who heals you'* (Exodus 15:26), to 'This is the water that healed me', 'This is the oil that healed me', and 'This is the prophet who healed me'.

Pursues Holiness

Jesus is coming for a Church that is separated for Him. A people that are consecrated for Him, devoted to Him. A people that do not replace Him for anything. Paul spoke harshly to the Galatians for moving away from the truth. *'O foolish Galatians! Who has bewitched you that you should not obey the truth, before whose eyes Jesus Christ was clearly portrayed among you as crucified?"* (Galatians 3:1).

There cannot be any other Christ crucified. There cannot be any other Christ who suffered 39 stripes for our healing. There cannot be any other Christ pierced and wounded for our transgressions and inequities. Ours is to take a decision that we cast our lot with the one and only Messiah, who is blessed and exalted forever.

Let Christ come and find a bride who is separated for Him and Him alone. Let Him find a people who will not replace Him on a whim. Let Him find a people who say like the Hebrew boys, *'O Nebuchadnezzar, we have no need to answer you in this matter. If that is the case, our God whom we serve is able to deliver us from the burning fiery furnace, and He will deliver us from your hand, O king. But if not, let it be known to you, O king, that we do not serve your gods, nor will we worship the gold image which you have set up.'* (Daniel 3:16–18).

Sometimes the furnace of problems in life seems like it has been heated seven times. It seems like there is no

The Bride of Jesus

end to the challenges we face. It seems like people who have no God are living a better life than we are, and that the solution is out there, but not with us. Yet I say to you, right there in the fiery furnace was a fourth man who was 'like a Son of God'. He was there for the young men who were separated for Him.

They were holy, devoted to the only true God. They would not defile themselves with the food of Babylon. They would not replace their God with a golden image of a man. They would rather die than bow to any other God. They were not desperate even when faced with the possibility of death in the fire. Desperation of facing the fire today makes some people to turn away from trusting God to trusting people and things. Just as the plate on the forehead of Aaron the priest was engraved with the words, *'Holiness to the LORD'* (Exodus 28:36), so, too, is the bride of Jesus so engraved. Be holy, therefore, and set apart for God.

8
Submits

'Wives, submit to your own husbands, as is fitting in the Lord. Husbands, love your wives and do not be bitter toward them' (Colossians 3:18–19).

The word 'submission' has been used and misused, often to justify the abuse of women. It has been so misapplied that many women now despise the word. When a man lords it over a woman, saying, 'You must submit to me!' his words may be met with resistance, because these are not pleasant words to hear and the manner in which they are uttered is often offensive.

Submission is the action of accepting or yielding to a superior force or to the will or authority of another person. It is an attitude that recognises and accepts the rights of authority.

The Bride of Jesus

The Bible reflects the patriarchal system which was prevalent in society during Bible times. I have read that when we read the Bible, we must determine whether it's precepts are cultural or normative, which means 'Is this verse describing a cultural practice, particular to that time and place, or is it describing a universal truth that applies to us all?' If we were to discern between these two, we would be able to find out the will of God concerning many specific issues.

This book is premised on the idea of the bride being the Church and the bridegroom being Jesus, which is how Jesus Himself put it. Just as a wife submits to her husband, so the Church must submit to Christ. The Bible makes it clear that a woman must submit to her husband, and her husband must love her.

Women at times say it is easier to submit to a loving husband. Submission comes easily when we are loved. When someone shows us love, protects us and honours us, we willingly to do as asked because we know they ask not out of a desire to dominate, but out of love.

When we look back at the original husband and wife, we see a blueprint of the relationship between man and woman, and God and Church. In the beginning, God created them male and female, and He brought them before Him, in whatever form they were, and blessed them both. He said, in essence, to both the male and the fe-

Submits

male, 'Dominate and rule over everything, not over each other, but over the earth, the animals and the birds of the sky.' Not once did God say to the male, 'Dominate and rule over the female', or to the female, 'Dominate and rule over the male.'

He gave both of them the authority to dominate and rule. That was the blessing, the first instruction. The things that were to submit under the authority of male and female were the earth and everything on it – animals, birds and fish.

Having formed the male first, it was to the man that God gave the instructions; He then made the woman out of the man. The man heard God's words directly, and the woman heard them indirectly, from the man. She also heard from him the instructions concerning the tree of the knowledge of good and evil, and was the first to be deceived. When she gave the man the fruit to eat, he disobeyed God and obeyed the woman. She had not heard the exact words of God, but he had.

God then pronounced His judgment upon the serpent, the man and the woman. He said to the woman, *'Your desire shall be for your husband, and he shall rule over you'* (Genesis 3:16).

In other words, God had blessed them to rule, but the relationship between the two was going to change;

the man would now rule over the woman. The ego of the man had been crushed, he had been led to disobedience, and his relationship with God had been broken. The result of his sin and the breaking of his bond with God was that the man would now rule over the woman, and the woman's desire would be for her husband.

We find that this norm prevails; a woman will look at a man and wish that he would marry her, but the man initiates the action. The husband rules. He is the one who approaches first, and she either welcomes his advances or she does not. This is the pattern that has been in place since man first sinned.

It is the rule of God that a man should submit to God. That submission was lost in the beginning because of sin. That submission no longer comes naturally, but has to be practised. Human beings have been trying to submit to God ever since Adam first broke that bond.

I have had my own run-ins with submission. It is not easy. At times we submit not because we agree, but because of the authority. If you agree, then that is agreement, not submission. Submission comes when there is a decision to be made and one person has to make it, and that decision becomes the rule.

Time and again I have had to swallow my own opinion and say it is fine, let it go and then go to the Father and say, 'Please deal with this matter.' There is not a single person on earth who is always right.

We all need the wisdom of God in the decisions we make. Sometimes the decision of the husband is wrong. Disagreeing about it will simply bring a fight. When it is a critical issue then it might be worth insisting on your viewpoint. If it is important but not critical, it might be worth submitting, and talking about it later. The small stuff, however, is not worth fighting for. At times you will be vindicated later. There is absolutely nothing wrong with going to God with your complaint, especially if you are sure that you are right.

Submission would not sound like a horrible thing if man and woman treated each other with love and respect. The woman would find it easy to respond in submission, for she is loved, she is cherished, she is not looked down upon, she is consulted, her viewpoint is considered important.

The relationship between us and Christ is one of submission. We believe the Son of God came in the flesh, we believe He died for our sins, we believe He is highly exalted and seated at the right hand of God the Father. Therefore we accept Him as our Lord, and therefore, what He says stands. It is for us to obey. We submit to Christ who first loved us.

The Bride of Jesus

The Bible says, 'Woman, submit; man, love.' This pattern applies as much to Jesus and the Church as it does to man and woman. Jesus first loved the world, and the people of God submit easily because they know they are loved.

Which woman would not want to submit to a man who died for her, a man who suffered for her healing, who was chastised for her peace, who was wounded for her transgressions, who was bruised for her inequities? There is no way you would want to defy a man who has done so much for you, whose actions have been all for your good, and whose love for you is endless. Jesus did everything out of love for us, and all He wants is that we submit to Him.

What are we submitting to? We are submitting to the way He wants us to live as citizens of His kingdom. When Jesus says, 'In my kingdom, we do things by prayer', we submit to that. It may not be easy at times. You may be tired, but because He said pray, you pray.

When He says, 'Love one another,' when He says, 'Love your enemies,' we ought to submit. We submit because He loved both us and His own enemies while we were sinners. We submit to the Lord Jesus when He says, 'Fellowship with one another,' when He says, 'Lay your hands on the sick' and when He says, 'You shall do greater things than these.'

Submits

We submit out of love and in a spirit of gratitude.

It is not easy to go and lay your hands on a sick person, because if they don't get well they may regard you as foolish. But He was whipped and crucified for our healing – *'by His stripes we are healed'* (Isaiah 53:5) – and when we lay our hands upon the sick, we do it out of submission to Him. The rest is up to Him.

In some marriages, the woman is prepared to submit to the pastor or to the servant of God more than she is prepared to submit to her husband. How can that be? The first institution that was established was marriage, which existed long before the Church. You cannot submit to your pastor and then fail to submit to your husband with whom you live and with whom you are in a covenant relationship. You cannot claim to submit to Christ if you will not submit to your husband; you are defying both Christ and your husband.

Submission does not mean you have to leave your intelligence outside the door when you get married. The first person we submit to is God. If there is anything asked of you that does not line up with the Word of God, then as respectfully as possible you present this to your husband. You may not kill a person out of submission to your husband, nor steal and lie.

The Bride of Jesus

That is why it is a fundamental thing for the husband to be submitted to God; if he lives in submission to God, then he will not ask or expect things of his wife that are contrary to God's will. If we were to look at Christ and behold the beauty of His holiness and the finished work of the cross, then we would not have to tell one another to obey the Word of God, or to live a godly life.

There would not be a need to tell one another to dress appropriately, to steer clear of adultery, to get married first, to be honest, to forgive our brethren, and not to hate. We would do all of these things out of love and gratitude to Christ. If we believe the Word of God, we ought to submit to Him. Our bridegroom is coming soon. It may be in a day or a thousand years, but He will come. When He comes, He is coming for a Church that submits to Him, not to the pressures of society.

People are now submitting to the clapping of hands and the cries of the congregation – 'Prophesy, man of God!' Then the man prophesy. Such men are not submitting to the Spirit of God, who may say, 'Sit down, I have no word for this person.' But because people are excited and demand prophecy, the servant of God submits to them instead of to God.

'And the L*ORD* *said to me, "The prophets prophesy lies in My name. I have not sent them, commanded them, nor spoken to them; they prophesy to you a false vi-*

sion, *divination, a worthless thing, and the deceit of their heart'* (Jeremiah 14:14).

The mistake that King Saul made was to submit to people instead of God. When they said, 'We are scared, we need a sacrifice,' Saul slaughtered an animal as a sacrifice, disobeying God's instruction that Samuel should make the sacrifice. When they said, 'We are hungry, we want to eat,' he said, 'Have all the fattened calves.' That was the downfall of Saul. A man who cannot submit to God but submits easily to human beings is not pleasing to God. God takes away certain things that He has given because of disobedience.

We are expected to submit to the Lord and to do as He says. His burden is light, His yoke is easy, and to serve God is not a difficult thing. If only we knew that what we will have and achieve is all wrapped up in the Lord, we would bow gracefully. None of our achievements are our doing. If I fail, having done everything that the Lord said I must do, then it is not I who has failed, but the Lord. But the Lord cannot fail. Then, indeed, it is I who has failed.

'Therefore submit to God. Resist the devil and he will flee from you' (James 4:7). May God help us to submit where submission is due; the woman to her husband, and the believer to the Lord.

9
Cared for

And my God shall supply all your need according to His riches in glory by Christ Jesus

(Philippians 4:19).

The one thing I told my husband when we got married was that, no matter how much I might earn during our marriage, as long as he was working, I expected to be fed by him. That for me is basic. Many will disagree with me because of feminist ideals.

I support those ideals. But I also love to be feminine and cared for. It is in me as a woman. Fortunately for me, I was working when we met. It was therefore not out of necessity that I said those words, but out of choice. He is to remain the main provider in the house. The money I earn I add to his.

The Bride of Jesus

We have done great things together in this way. For the husband to provide the basic necessities is a fundamental principle.

I want to be cared for. I am not demanding unreasonable amounts here, only basic care. I already had a degree and was working when we met.

It is built into the system of a man to be a provider. He wants to feel wanted and needed, which is quite different from being a control freak. A normal man wants to care for his wife and children. The little or plenty that he earns should be sufficient to feed the family. The challenge comes when both partners want to raise the standard of living; in that case, the wife must play a financial role.

I can never take away the responsibility that my husband has to feed and care for us, but should he be unable to, I am not helpless. I already work with my hands and brain, and would be able to step in and fill the gap should the need arise.

When God put man in the Garden of Eden, the plants and fruits were already there for him to eat. He did not have to wait to plant and harvest; instead, God provided for him. When the woman shifted her position and entertained the serpent concerning food, she was deceived. She was not there when God gave instructions concerning the food arrangements, but received these from her husband. It was his responsibility to identify the food to be eaten and the one tree from which they were both not to eat.

I acknowledge that things have changed. Women are frequently equal or greater providers than their husbands are. But earning more than your husband does not make you the man of the house, as the principle of submission has nothing to do with money. I am for equality in marriage, as we are clearly both made in the image of God. After Adam sinned, God said:

'Cursed is the ground for your sake; in toil you shall eat of it all the days of your life. Both thorns and thistles it shall bring forth for you, and you shall eat the herb of the field. In the sweat of your face you shall eat bread till you return to the ground' (Genesis 3:17–19).

Sweating and toiling is not nice. Doing what I love and being paid for it, now that is more to my taste. But we take our cue from the Proverbs 31 woman, who wakes up, allocates work to her servants and goes out to make money. There is no need to go back to the Dark Ages. Boardrooms are brighter with our faces and brains there, and we should not underplay what God has given us. However, for all the excellence we bring, we are women and believers, and the principle of the man as main provider applies. Let us look now at the bride of Jesus. Jesus on earth was a carpenter's son. Culture would dictate that He was a carpenter too, although the Bible does not specifically say that He followed in His earthly father's footsteps.

We see a pattern that as man, he worked and was a provider, a pattern learned from Joseph. When Jesus began to minister, He performed miracles of provision. He multiplied a few fish and loaves of bread so that He could feed thousands of people who were hungry. The disciples had in mind to send the crowd away after they had heard the preaching, but Jesus, Good Shepherd that He is, had compassion and saw it as His responsibility to provide for their physical needs as well as their spiritual needs.

Jesus met many different hungry people in the three years of His ministry, and did not feed them all. I believe He wanted to reveal a quality of God here; that God is our provider. If He could feed so many with the little food that was available, He can certainly feed a few with whatever they bring.

The principle of bringing a little something when you want something more is biblical. God will use what you have to put more into your basket or barn. The only time where provision came out of nothing was when God rained down manna from heaven in the wilderness.

Cared for

All the Israelites had to do was show up with their baskets and receive the food. When Elijah was hungry, God used ravens to bring food to where he was hiding. When the brook dried up, he went to a widow and requested that she provide him with a meal. She did, and the little she gave was replenished again and again until the famine was over.

When a widow whose husband's creditors came to take her sons as payment, she went to the prophet and put her case before him. Her husband had served under the prophet, and she called on him for help. He asked her what she had, and she said she had nothing but a little oil. That little oil was sufficient to get her out of debt. Elisha told her to get all the jars in the village, go home, close the door and pour her oil into the jars, little as it was. She did that, and filled all the jars until there was not one left empty – then the oil ceased. She sold all that oil and paid her creditors.

God controls the universe. He made water gush from a rock so His thirsty people could drink. He changed water into wine so that people could be merry. He can multiply whatever you have in your hands to meet your needs.

Paul wrote to the Philippians that they were generous in their offering. He was not desperate for food, but wanted them to understand the principle of giving and then receiving, not receiving and then receiving more. After they had given, Paul released a blessing upon them, saying that God would meet their needs according to His riches in glory by Christ Jesus.

Many servants of God live by faith and tell stories of traveling to minister wherever God calls them, even when they have no money. They live on the provision of God. John G Lake came to South Africa, received provision for the journey, and on arrival at the harbour, found a lady waiting to take them to a home prepared for him and his family. She was a stranger to them, and they to her. This is the provision of God.

If the bride of Jesus could come to a full realisation of Jesus' unlimited power, such miracles would be common.

Giving should never involve forcing people to part with what they don't have and do not wish to give. In such cases, there is human interference, and faith is lacking. If all the giving we see these days in the Church was truly of faith, then there would be more miracles of provision.

There is a connection between giving and receiving. If it is of God, there is a return. Yet our reason for giving should not be the return we seek for ourselves but about the life of obedience we have committed to. I re-

Cared for

cently went to an event. I had money enough for petrol to get me there and back and to pay the road toll. I went to minister there. I did not pay for exhibition space as I did not have that money. I took a few books with me, simply as a reference and to show those some few people.

When I arrived, the host asked if I had brought my books, then gave me exhibition space – quite unexpected as I did make a booking. By the time I left, I had sold a lot of books and made three times the amount I had used to travel with. I must confess that I did not pray for this provision. I just took what I had and used it for the mission of God. I did not 'call for money' or anything – I just put my last money down and brought what I had. I did not worry about my lack, about not even having enough for a cup of tea on the two-hour journey.

On my way back I glorified God for His faithfulness. I saw myself living the scripture that says, *'Therefore do not worry, saying, "What shall we eat?" or "What shall we drink?" or "What shall we wear?" ... For your heavenly Father knows that you need all these things. But seek first the kingdom of God and His righteousness, and all these things shall be added to you'* (Matthew 6:31–32).

I must say that this experience was not because I move in faith in a great way, but only because God was at work, and by His grace gave me this experience so that I could learn. Henceforth I could live by faith, or return to worrying. By His grace I am learning to live by faith.

The disciples did not have to worry about food for themselves. Jesus had concern for both their spiritual and physical needs. The righteous are never forsaken. Nor do the righteous ever forsake others.

The early Church understood the principle of caring for one another. *'Now the multitude of those who believed were of one heart and one soul; neither did anyone say that any of the things he possessed was his own, but they had all things in common ... And great grace was upon them all. Nor was there anyone among them who lacked; for all who were possessors of lands or houses sold them, and brought the proceeds of the things that were sold, and laid them at the apostles' feet; and they distributed to each as anyone had need'* (Acts 4:32–35).

Jesus taught His disciples to care for people and to share what they had. A young boy shared his little lunch with a multitude of people. The disciples shared their lunch with the multitude also. This Kingdom is one of giving, sharing the Good News and constant provision. Dorcas cared for the widows and the orphans, providing them with blankets and clothes. She was a giver who sought no reward, and at her death did not need anyone to extol her virtues; her works spoke on her behalf. The people called for Peter to raise her from the dead. He came, and she was raised up.

Cared for

The Church has focused on giving one person instead of sharing generously with one other. Believers seek wealth for themselves in giving to one person, expecting a blessing in return. This is contrary to the spirit of the early Church, whose giving was amongst one another.

Jesus is coming to a Church that gives, and that does so willingly, because of the pattern He has established for us. He gave more than any of us ever could – His own life for the people.

The bride of Jesus is cared for by her husband. He has provided the power to change every troubling situation.

10
Empowered

'But you shall receive power when the Holy Spirit has come upon you; and you shall be witnesses to Me in Jerusalem, and in all Judea and Samaria, and to the end of the earth' (Acts 1:8).

The one thing God gave to men is physical strength and the responsibility to protect their wives. We can cry equality all we want, but when it comes to certain things, they are better done by men. There are exceptions, of course, of women who are physically stronger than men, but this is not the norm.

A few years ago a thief entered our house while we were sleeping. I had just given birth, and was a light sleeper. I woke up at the sound of movement in the room, and woke my husband. While he took his time in waking, the thief escaped through the window. When my husband

The Bride of Jesus

realised that I was not dreaming, and that a thief had really been inside our bedroom, the thought that his wife and child could have been hurt while he was there distressed him greatly. He is the protector of his family. As a husband and father he would rather fight for his family than see them hurt. God has given him physical strength for that.

While on this earth Jesus did many mighty miracles, signs and wonders. He displayed the power of God to the demonic spirits that possessed the men of Gadarene. He had power over sickness that had held people captive for many years – 38 years, in the case of the lame man at the pool of Bethesda, 12 years for the woman with an issue of blood and 18 years for the bent woman in the temple. He had power over the water, the waves and the wind. He had power to multiply food and feed thousands.

The disciples of Jesus walked with Him and witnessed all these things. Naturally, any person would wish to have a similar power and to perform similar miracles.

The amazing thing about the Kingdom is that it is not centred on one person; it is for us all, and centred on Jesus. Everyone is expected to contribute and be involved. Jesus gave the disciples power and sent them out to preach the Good News, to heal the sick and cast out demons. The disciples could do nothing special before Jesus – some were just fishermen, and nothing spectacular.

Empowered

They knew nothing about a man born blind being able to see. Meeting with Jesus opened their eyes to a world of impossibilities becoming possible.

A dead man waking up and walking out of the tomb after four days? That was a first for them. Such power was made available for them, too. Jesus sent them out with power. Yet even with the authority they had, they failed to cast a demon out of a certain child. It must have frustrated them – the crowd looking on and seeing them fail to do what was easy for their Lord. It must have reminded them just how human and limited they were. As with many of us, Jesus was not with them at that point. When He came and the father cried out to Jesus, the child was delivered.

When He was about to leave this earth, Jesus told the disciples that He was not leaving them helpless. He left them with power to preach, cast out demons and heal the sick. Empowered by the Holy Spirit, the Apostle Peter set out to the temple and met a crippled man who regularly begged at the same spot.

Peter must have passed that spot many times before, but this time, he had something to give the man. He had power to heal in the name of Jesus. He ordered the man to arise, and as he spoke, the power of God surged through the man's crippled limbs, and he arose and took his first step. In fact he leaped with excitement and went into the temple praising God.

Such power! The disciples were never the same after receiving the power of the Holy Spirit. The same Peter who had denied Jesus three times only weeks before was then bold enough to stand and speak about Jesus, despite huge opposition. Fear was defeated by the power of God. When a young man fell and died from the house in which the apostle Paul was preaching, he went down and woke him up.

Jesus did not leave a lame duck bride. He left a powerful force of saints that would go out and turn the world upside down. The people who were proud to have rid the world of Jesus had a new nemesis. He had multiplied Himself in His bride, the Church. She was on earth representing Him, doing the things He did, and more. *'Most assuredly, I say to you, he who believes in Me, the works that I do he will do also; and greater works than these he will do, because I go to My Father'* (John 14:12).

And the disciples indeed did many greater works. In the years since, many servants of God have followed His path and performed many signs and wonders. Of note, I am inspired by the ministry of Kathryn Kuhlman, Maria Woodworth-Etter, John G Lake and Lester Sumrall. I have read books about the amazing miracles done by God through these servants. Cancer, tuberculosis, arthritis, blindness, demoniacs, crippled and dying people were healed by the power of God working through them.

Maria Woodwoth-Etter — what miracles were wrought in the ministry of this woman. From being a housewife content with staying at home and raising her children, then losing them one by one, she arose to preach healing. That took boldness in the Spirit. She did not sit and wallow in self-pity for the children she had lost. She went out and preached healing, preferring that people be saved from sickness than mourn for her children. People were healed and glorified God.

Kathryn Kuhlman preached mostly about the Holy Spirit, bringing to light the importance and the role of this aspect of God. She would pray until she was filled, then ascend the stage and miracles would happen. She acknowledged the role of the Holy Spirit, saying that if we lived and died without meeting her, we would not have missed a thing, but that we had to meet the Holy Spirit.

We can learn from her about lifting the Lord rather than ourselves. With all her imperfections, she had a heart sold out for the Lord. She is proof that indeed God qualifies the ones He chooses. And from the ones He chooses God expects much, since he has given much. Such power!

When John G Lake came to South Africa and

preached the Gospel, many healings were recorded. His convictions about healing were so strong that he had no fear of coming into contact with contagious diseases. Jesus, too, touched the leprous man without fear of contracting the disease.

Lester Sumrall taught about the gifts of the Holy Spirit. His teaching brought understanding, ignited people and propelled change. He sought to see many people empowered to do the works that Jesus did. He emphasised that the gifts manifest where they are desired, expected, known and given space to function. We cannot grieve the Holy Spirit and expect Him to move mightily in our midst.

Some churches have dimmed the light of the Holy Spirit. Like the religious leaders of old, they say, *'He casts out demons by the ruler of the demons'* (Matthew 9:34). They say they do not believe in miracles. The offence of the false prophets has caused some to deny the power of God because of the few who misuse the Word of God for personal gain. Few are prepared to *'test the spirits, whether they are of God'* (1 John 4:1). Rather, they deny all works, whether they are from God or not.

Denying the miracles that God can do is like taking a long distance flight and refusing to eat the food offered in flight. You would rather reach your destination hungry and thirsty because you are focused on getting

Empowered

there. Well-fed or hungry, you will get there. Isn't it better to reach your destination nourished and not thirsty?

Some believers are afraid of casting out demons. They do not want to be touched by someone with a visible manifestation of what they do not understand. Some have missed God while running away from the devil. People come to church today and go home the same as they were because the church is not prepared to use the power that is available.

The lame in the Church need the power that was available and operating in Peter when he met the lame man at the gate called Beautiful. They need no silver or gold, but a hand that will hold them up in the name of Jesus so that they may rise and walk. The Day of Pentecost is needed in the Church, where everyone is filled with the Holy Spirit and in one accord stand against evil forces.

The sick in Church and in the hospitals need the power that caused the sick in Peter's path to line up so that his shadow would fall on them and they would be healed. People trust the water and the oil and in many cases run away from the real power that heals. People would rather die than approach the hem of Christ's garment like the woman with the issue of blood.

The demon you are afraid of because it is manifesting is less to be feared than the one who remains hidden and operational in someone's life. There are demons that are mute in church, sitting down with all decorum, even worshipping together with you, hugging you as the Pastor says, 'Greet each other with a holy kiss,' and you think the person is normal because you don't see any manifestation.

Some people come to church to do witchcraft, to bring down the pastor, take away membership and put out the Spirit's fire. They come in sheep's clothing and find a lame duck kind of church that cannot discern spirits. A church that does not know the potential power that is available to cast out demons is at the mercy of the demons they fear.

Jesus released the power we need on the Day of Pentecost. The Bible makes no mention of this power coming to an end. The Holy Spirit will continue working until Jesus comes, but He can only operate where He is acknowledged. The men of Ephesus believed, but knew only the baptism of John. When they were preached to and baptised, the power of God came upon them. *'And when Paul had laid hands on them, the Holy Spirit came upon them, and they spoke with tongues and prophesied'* (Acts 19:6).

They believed. They lacked the power. They received and began prophesying. The Bible does not say that only their leader prophesied. They all prophesied.

Empowered

They did not wait to go to Bible College before they prophesied. They were not prophets, but they prophesied. They received the power and they used it immediately. Did they make mistakes? We don't know. All we are told is that they were empowered and they functifoned.

The power of God should not lie dormant while the people of God struggle, waiting passively for Jesus to come back. He left us with His power so we can be fruitful while He is preparing to come back.

Could the Church today come to the point where liars like Ananias and Sapphira are exposed? Where Simon the sorcerer is exposed and delivered? The Church needs to begin to hear God sending individuals out to minister instead of confining potential ministers to the local church. The harvest is out there – we need to look outward and not inward.

'Now God worked unusual miracles by the hands of Paul' (Acts 19:11). For the Bible to mention 'unusual' miracles, there must have usual miracles, too. Imagine fellowshipping with people where it is a usual thing to heal the sick, and where from time to time God does something unusual or spectacular.

That is the bride Jesus is coming for. The kind that has risen in the power of the Holy Ghost and put the little devils in their place, far away from their homes, their places of fellowship, their workplaces. The bride of Jesus is empowered to do these things, and even more.

Jesus was never selfish. He wanted all of us to reign on this earth. Dominion has long been given to man; it was given at the beginning. Having lost our power through sin, God restored it again through salvation.

Live in the way the Lord is calling you to.

When you have received the power, do not sit on it; use it.

When more are empowered, rejoice. 'Two can chase ten thousand.'

11
Must be ready

'And while they went to buy, the bridegroom came, and those who were ready went in with him to the wedding; and the door was shut' (Matthew 25:10).

Brides are known to be fashionably late to their own weddings. Waking up early, the bride frets over every little detail, and her desire to look perfect on her wedding eventually causes her to be late. Some even come hours late, leaving their guests waiting, sometimes not so patiently. The sad thing is that the bride who does this robs herself by being so late; the people who are meant to celebrate her special day end up rushed and harassed, as the director of the programme tries to catch up. The best thing a bride can do is to be ready and on time for her own wedding.

The Bride of Jesus

The parable of the ten virgins presents a different view of a wedding setting. Here, the virgins are waiting for the bridegroom. He is late and they grow tired of waiting, and fall asleep. That is not typical of brides – how can they relax and fall asleep before the bridegroom arrives? In this case, they have waited until they can wait no longer, and fall asleep.

Each virgin has her own lamp as she waits. Five of the virgins run out of oil and then the bridegroom arrives. They are not ready. They need oil and the only people who can possibly assist are the other five virgins. They ask to share the oil, but the wise ones refuse. If they share, they may run out of oil themselves and then there will be no light. The wise virgins advise the foolish ones to buy their own oil. While the foolish virgins are out, the bridegroom arrives, and the foolish ones miss out on the wedding.

After all the preparations, the dressing up, and the waiting, the foolish ones have missed the most important detail; their lamps were supposed to be continually lit. How can they participate in the wedding without their lamps? What has darkness to do with light? How can there be a wedding in darkness?

That the Lord Jesus is coming back is not in question; it is a matter of time. *'It is not for you to know times or seasons which the Father has put in His own authority'*

Must be ready

(Acts 1:7). The length of time the Lord is taking in coming back has been a snare for many people. Unbelievers hold it against Christianity, treating it as an old wives' tale. Some believers slowly move back into complacency, thinking Jesus is late.

Jesus, in responding to His disciples, did not correct them for believing that the Messianic kingdom was coming. He corrected their assumption that it was possible to know when the Kingdom would come. He made it clear that it could be at any time.

Instead of being bogged down by arguments over the time of the Kingdom's arrival, Jesus refocused His disciples on the work at hand, which was to witness worldwide about the coming Kingdom. The Gospel had to be preached to the whole world. It is not a matter of waiting for Christ to return, but of preparing for the return of Christ. He must find a people for His Kingdom.

Jesus then brought them to the enablement for this worldwide ministry – power. He was sending them out to work with power, in order to do great exploits. In the Old Testament, the Holy Spirit is represented by oil.

The story of the virgins illustrates the truth that the Holy Spirit is required in our lives while we wait for the Lord's return. You do not wait with lamps that are dry. You keep the lamp burning with oil. The Holy Spirit is that oil; He gives light. He exposes falsehoods such as those expressed by Ananias and Sapphira and He also provides light for the paths of His followers, so that we know which way to go. The light will reveal who needs help and who should be brought to salvation.

Instead of sitting around arguing about whether days, years or centuries might still elapse before Jesus comes, we should be doing the work of the Lord. In any case, to God a day is like a thousand years, and a thousand years is like a day. God is not bound by time.

The problem with focusing on when Jesus is coming back is that this wrong focus leads to discouragement, with people wanting to live for the 'now'. The virgins went back to sleep, planning to wake up when He came, but when He came, they were not ready. The sinner continues sinning, thinking he has enough time to catch up with salvation. The enemy deceives many into thinking they have endless time. Death, however, comes unexpectedly.

People are ticking the register of the church as present while the heavenly register is not ticked. They are in church every Sunday, give generously, and participate in church activities, but their hearts are not right with God. Servants of God have a responsibility to look beyond the generous gifts from people, the souls must be brought to Christ. The number of people in attendance is not as important as the ones that receive salvation. It is always joyous when an altar call is made and persons who have been coming to church for a long time go forward to give their lives to Christ.

The Church is not a parking space for those temporarily passing. The Church is a place where sinners are brought to the foot of the cross. People must be cut to the core until they ask, *'Men and brethren, what shall we do?'* (Acts 2:37). Then they must be told, *'Repent, and let every one of you be baptized in the name of Jesus Christ for the remission of sins; and you shall receive the gift of the Holy Spirit. For the promise is to you and to your children, and to all who are afar off, as many as the Lord our God will call'* (Acts 2:38).

People should not be given membership forms because they have come to church. They must be led to Jesus first and foremost, and be taught about the principles of this Kingdom. Then they will be ready to commit themselves to constant fellowship with the brethren. It should never be about the numbers but about the condition of the souls. Jesus told a parable of a man who thought he had time to enjoy the fruits of his labour. At an unforeseen hour, death struck. God said to him, *'Fool! This night your soul will be required of you; then whose will those things be which you have provided?'* (Luke 12:20).

The Bride of Jesus

It is indeed foolish to think we have control over our own lives. It is foolish to think there is time enough to get saved. Do not trample on the blood that was spilled on Calvary. Jesus is coming back. Even if He does not come tomorrow, you might go to the grave tomorrow and have no chance of making right with Him.

The bride cannot afford to start looking for her shoes when the time of the wedding comes. Many times a bride has had to do without items she wanted. When we had our wedding anniversary celebration, we reached the venue a bit late, and the sound was not as sorted as we wanted. I got out of the car and said, 'We will do with what is available.' There was no time to go to the merchants – the time for the feast had come.

Jesus wants to find a bride waiting for Him. She must be radiant, filled with glory. She must have triumphed over the enemy and remained standing. She must have brought light into the world. She must be clothed in fine apparel, wearing perfume and emanating a sweet fragrance, which is the prayers of the saints going up to heaven. She cannot afford to slumber. The enemy crouches in the night. Her lamp must shine brightly, continuously.

The clock is ticking.

12

Glorious

'Husbands, love your wives, just as Christ also loves the church and gave Himself for her, that He might sanctify and cleanse her with the washing of water by the word, that He might present her to Himself a glorious church, not having spot or wrinkle or any such thing, but that she should be holy and without blemish' (Ephesians 5:25–27).

A bride always has a glow about her, deserving the title 'most beautiful person in the room'. She is radiant, looks good, smells good and feels good. It is such joy for her on that day to be the centre of attention. The dress is carefully selected, fits perfectly. Her face is polished nicely, all the blemishes removed, for her skin has been prepared for months. She is looking beautiful for her husband.

The Bride of Jesus

Esther, the young Jewish girl in the book of Esther, went through a whole year of preparation before being selected as the bride of the king. He wanted the best queen for the kingdom. They used oils and perfumes to prepare the girls for the day that they would appear before the king. They had to look radiant and beautiful. She went in and was selected to fill the important role of being wife to the king, queen in the kingdom. She was glorious.

Spots and blemishes are signs that something is wrong with the skin or inside the body. Some people get them when they eat sugar. Some have various skin conditions. Some react to stress with a breakout of pimples or other changes in their skin. To deal with bad skin conditions, cleansing and nourishing is done. Some need treatments that must be drunk in order to deal with the issue from the inside. Some may simply be told to rest in order for their skin to clear up.

The Church that Jesus is coming for is one without spot, wrinkle or blemish. Jesus is coming to a Church that has no issues that might give rise to scorn. You cannot live in sin as a believer and expect not to have spiritual 'spots'. People see these and begin to doubt your salvation or Jesus Himself because of the spots they see in you.Blemishes show that something is not right inside. People need to heal, people need to mature.

Glorious

In the scripture above, note that it is the husband, Christ, who washes the bride, the Church. He washes her by the Word. It is the Word that brings about holiness. For when the believer is soaked in the Word, eventually fornication falls off, the urge to drink goes away, anger disappears. She begins to glow, and she lives by the scripture that reminds her to sing, *'I will praise You, for I am fearfully and wonderfully made; marvelous are your works, and that my soul knows very well'* (Psalm 139:14). She begins to looks at herself differently, her self-esteem reaches an all-time high, and she appreciates herself.

When the Church begins to appreciate the Word, no one worries about what they will eat or wear. They are filled with joy, and bring their requests to God, resting in His promises. Worry adds years to your face. To start glowing, stop worrying.

The bridegroom sanctifies His bride, separating her from all others. He makes her His own. All this is done by the Word. As soon as she believes that her Lord is God and there is no other, she stops trusting anyone and anything but Jesus. She gives herself to Him wholeheartedly. In no time, she comes to the point of blessing the Lord, *'... who satisfies your mouth with good things, so that your youth is renewed like the eagle's'* (Psalm 103:5). Who would not be glorious when her youth is renewed? Who renews but God? How else does He renew but with the Word?

The Bride of Jesus

Jesus is coming for a bride who is without spot. God is holy, and expects us to be holy. A bride whose white dress gets stained with a big black mark before she walks down the aisle will definitely be touched by sadness. A dark spot can only come out through soaking and rigorous washing. How can the spots in our lives be removed without soaking in the Word of God?

Wrinkles are a result of old age, and come to the young through worry and stress. A bride who is always worried before her wedding day may end up with dark circles under her eyes which will need to be camouflaged with make-up. There is no make-up in this world that will cover up spiritual wrinkles.

You greet such a person and all you hear is that the weather is bad, the economy is bad, the spouse is giving them a headache, the bank account has a zero balance, the children are ungrateful, the church is not helping ... on and on, about all the things that are wrong in the world. Yet Jesus has given us power over all things, and has given us His Word, His Spirit, and the assurances of salvation. None of this has ever diminished, but we just do not grasp it.

Granted, the issues we face daily can weigh us down. Sometimes the bank account seems to be hitting a continuous zero. When King David reached a state of sadness, he roused himself and said, *'Why are you cast down, O my soul? And why are you disquieted within me?'* (Psalm 43:5).

It was a time of reflection. He had been through great troubles, and his soul had reached a low point. Instead of finding someone else to lift his spirits, David sought the answer within. *'Hope in God; for I shall yet praise Him, the help of my countenance' (*Psalm 43:5). It takes a mental move away from your situation and into the presence of God for worrying issues to become less significant. You sit praising God, although the solution is not even manifest yet.

It is Christ glorified who raises a believer to glory. *'To them God willed to make known what are the riches of the glory of this mystery among the Gentiles: which is Christ in you, the hope of glory'* (Colossians 1:27). Our hope is not in our ability to resolve our own problems. Elijah did mighty things – he called fire down from heaven and boldly opposed kings – but there came a time in his life that he was so tired and discouraged that only God could help him. It is always Jesus in us who is our hope of glory.

'When Christ who is our life appears, then you also will appear with Him in glory' (Colossians 3:4). The first message the Lord gave me when He called me was that He was coming back for:

The Bride of Jesus

'... a bride that radiates the glory of the Lord, the beauty of His holiness. A bride that submits and is led by the Lord. No mixed-up messages and split allegiance. Our God is a jealous God, He will not share His glory. Let the bride adorn herself with fine apparel, the covering of the Lord, and a sweet perfume, which is the prayer of the saints. Let the bride be ready for her husband. Christ is coming soon.' 03 November 2012.

'I will greatly rejoice in the Lord, *my soul shall be joyful in my* God; For *He has clothed me with the garments of salvation, He has covered me with the robe of righteousness, as a bridegroom decks himself with ornaments, and as a bride adorns herself with her jewels'* (Isaiah 61:10).

What a joyous time it will be, when the bride of Jesus goes to meet her groom arrayed with the garment of salvation. She was long subject to death because of sin. But she has been born again, and covered with a new garment. She no longer has spots on her garment, but wears a robe of righteousness.

That is the bride Jesus is coming for.

13
Manifests the Lord

'For the earnest expectation of the creation eagerly waits for the revealing of the sons of God'

(Romans 8:19).

The mystery in a marriage is that two people who are totally different begin to live as one, and over the passage of time some begin to like the same things. There is a reason that God said a man must cleave to his wife. Cleaving allows for deep connection. The new family begins to chart their own future together without the influence of the parents. They decide what kind of home they will have, the number of children they would like, where they will live, the church they will attend, and so on.

The two individuals who make up the couple slowly begin to identify with one another. What has been agreed upon becomes law in their home. If the mirror is moved

The Bride of Jesus

from its usual place, the other will immediately see that something is different. In ways and ideas, they begin to reflect each other. This is spiritual connectedness, hidden from the world but manifested in society through their behaviour. People get to know that in that house, they live in a particular way. When the children are born, they become aligned with what has been established.

Some families are known for their kindness. You get to know one family member and you will be treated with kindness by all in the family. They are raised like that. I know of a dear family; when you walk in, even if you are in a hurry and just want to greet, everyone will come out and greet you, even the father and mother. You are not allowed to leave without eating food. As a friend to one, you are automatically a friend to the whole family. The children represent their parents well because they were taught well.

In like fashion, believers represent Christ in this world. When we see a true believer, we see, or should see, the character of Christ. We are in a process of becoming like Christ. *'But we all, with unveiled face, beholding as in a mirror the glory of the Lord, are being transformed into the same image from glory to glory, just as by the Spirit of the Lord'* (2 Corinthians 3:18).

Transformation is change; something has become something else over time. You cannot have Jesus and not become like Him. The key in the above scripture is 'beholding'. As you behold, you study, you accept as truth and you emulate. The disciples had different characters when Jesus met them. There were those who wanted the best position – to sit on the right or left of Jesus. There was Peter who was quick to answer, quick to act and to fight. There was Thomas who was full of doubt. They all beheld Jesus for three and half years and eventually became like Him.

'And the disciples were first called Christians in Antioch' (Acts 11:26).

There was something about these men that was evidence that they belonged to 'the way', as it was called then. The verses before the above scripture do not record miracles, but only that the disciples preached, that the hand of the Lord was with them, that people believed and that a great number was added to them. When Jesus went about preaching, a great multitude of people followed. As His disciples did what He had done, the rate at which the Church grew was notable. People realised that only Jesus had been able to pull off such things, and that these men must be Christians.

Jesus always confounded the educated religious people with His teachings and responses to issues. When they brought a woman caught in the act of adultery, they enquired of the Teacher what should be done. If Jesus said, 'Stone her in accordance with the Law of Moses,' then He was not truly preaching compassion and forgiveness. If He said, 'Forgive her,' then He was not obeying the Law of Moses. Jesus, however, handed the baton to them; the one who had no sin was to cast the first stone. They could either forgive her or stone her, depending on their own consciences. Perfect response.

When the disciples were arrested for preaching the Gospel and given an opportunity to respond, they gave answers that were on a par with the wisdom of Jesus. Their answers were so full of wisdom, the religious leaders took notice:

'Now when they saw the boldness of Peter and John, and perceived that they were uneducated and untrained men, they marveled. And they realized that they had been with Jesus' (Acts 4:13). Jesus' mission was accomplished. He had managed to replicate Himself on earth through men and women who would take Him to the world.

'For as many of you as were baptized into Christ have put on Christ' (Galatians 3:27). It is Christ who must be revealed in us. Our self has proven to be sinful in thoughts and in action. There is one who is completely pleasing to the Father, and that is the Son whom we are called to put on. It is a process of putting off the old man and putting on the new man who is in Christ.

Manifests the Lord

'My little children, for whom I labour in birth again until Christ is formed in you' (Galatians 4:19). When Christ is formed in us, *'... it is no longer I who live, but Christ lives in me; and the life which I now live in the flesh I live by faith in the Son of God, who loved me and gave Himself for me'* (Galatians 2:20). The bride has a responsibility to represent the family well wherever she goes. People are quick to say 'your wife' did this and that, instead of calling her by her name. The marriage institution fuses two people into one. When they see the wife they see the family. She represents her husband. She has his surname.

Being part of the bride of Jesus is not just about taking the name 'Christian'. The relationship between a believer and Christ is not just about a change in one person. Christianity does not end with you being saved. There is a bigger responsibility to being a Christian.

Christ said, 'You are the salt.' Salt brings taste to food. Food is not enjoyable without a bit of salt. People should want to eat the food you offer them – it should be tasty. Likewise, salvation should be attractive to people – they must want it as one wants tasty food. *'Oh, taste and see that the Lord is good; blessed is the man who trusts in Him!'* (Psalm 34:8).

Salvation should not be presented as a religion of rules, its product being poor, hungry, sick and downtrod-

The Bride of Jesus

den people. He became poor that we may be rich, in the full sense of the word. When we present a gospel of being okay with poverty, stress and strain, then Jesus became poor in vain. Then we look down on the sacrifice Jesus made for us. He could have been born in a mansion, and lived off the gold and silver at His disposal. He could have forgotten about us here on earth.

He was wounded for our healing. Imagine Him looking at all His wounds and then at us, living and accepting lives of sickness and poverty. What was the point of Jesus suffering so much pain, if we are not to claim His healing and His victory? Who are we representing here?

Imagine the ambassador of a rich country going to another country and presenting a poor image of his home. Who would want to go to a country which is badly represented by their ambassadors?

'Now then, we are ambassadors for Christ, as though God were pleading through us: we implore you on Christ's behalf, be reconciled to God' (2 Corinthians 5:20).

Ambassadors speak on behalf of their country of origin. They cannot speak against the law of their country. They cannot create their own laws in a foreign country. They represent the interests of their own country. They will not choose a foreign country over their country of

Manifests the Lord

origin. Countries whose policies clash with the policies of the host country are known to recall their ambassadors. The country of origin does not want their ambassador staying where there are major and significant differences of policies and values.

If a host country ignores calls to deal with child slavery within its borders, for example, the ambassador of another country may be recalled in order not to be seen to agree with this horrific practice.

The bride of Jesus is the ambassador of Christ on this earth. She abides by the law of her true country, which is heaven. She is indeed a heavenly citizen, and bound by what heaven prescribes. She also represents all that the kingdom of heaven has to offer. She cannot represent God who owns silver and gold and a cattle on a thousand hills by being content with having no silver or gold and even cattle. An ambassador is provided for by their own country. An official house and car is provided. The government pays for the ambassador to host guests at the official residence. Allowing ambassadors to struggle financially in a host country would give a bad name to the country that has deployed them.

The bride of Jesus – that is, the believers in Christ – are the sons of God. What a contrast in relationships; we are both bride and sons. Yet both positions are rooted in the Word of God. Nothing else created in this world is honoured with the privilege of being 'like God'. Look in the mirror – not at your physical attributes, but at the essence of your being – God is what you see. A human being is capable of being like God. People must see you and declare, 'God is alive.'

'For the earnest expectation of the creation eagerly waits for the revealing of the sons of God' (Romans 8:19). What does creation see in the Christians of today? Can they truly say, 'These are the sons of God?'

Jesus is a peacemaker. The Church is full of trouble makers. Social media is full of believers who make no peace, but want to show themselves more anointed and more powerful than others. Creation is watching and rejecting these. Creation says, 'These are not like Christ.' When Jesus was compared to John the Baptist, He walked away. He did not strive to prove the point that He was 'the one to come' whom John had spoken about. He did not want to grieve John after all the hard work he had been doing.

Jesus forgives, and He demonstrated that by forgiving those who nailed Him to the cross. He allowed Judas to sit close to Him on the table though He knew that he would betray Him. He also entrusted him with the money bag though he stole money from it. He preached and lived a life of forgiveness. He said forgive those who offend you seventy times seven.

Manifests the Lord

The church can be unforgiving of those who make mistakes. Some are scorned and talked about. They will crucify you for the sins that Jesus forgave you. This is not a reflection of Christ crucified and resurrected.

Jesus expects a people that live together in harmony and with love for one another. He is not coming for individuals that are self-seeking.

Servants of God today are giving themselves titles that are not even found in the Bible, all to present themselves as better than others. Not even Elijah who called down fire, or Elisha who obtained a double portion of the anointing, or Isaiah whose work still amazes us today were called anything other than prophet. The things that are happening in the body of Christ today are mindboggling. If there is anything that the world needs right now, it is Jesus.

When they search for Jesus they find man instead – pompous, and thinking of himself more highly than he ought to. Yet the people are saying, *'Sir, we wish to see Jesus'* (John 12:21).

14
Loved

'For God so loved the world that He gave His only begotten Son, that whoever believes in Him should not perish but have everlasting life' (John 3:16).

'In this the love of God was manifested toward us, that God has sent His only begotten Son into the world, that we might live through Him'

(1 John 4:9).

Women have many stories to tell of how they are proposed by men. The simple trick is, and always will be, 'I love you.' All other approaches are just empty or fancy pick-up lines (pardon me, brothers). Although the foundation for marriage runs deeper than mere words, nevertheless these three words have established relationships.

The Bride of Jesus

Many have walked down the aisle because of the unlocking power of these words, sincerely meant.

No matter what other words may be said, any serious person wants to come to the point where true love is expressed. 'I like you' does not cut it. It is love we seek and want to keep. Love is the motive behind acts of kindness and generosity towards another person. Love is not a feeling – it is expressed in words and deeds.

The story of the Bible is a love story, telling of the love of the Creator for the object of His creation. When God had created all things, He looked at everything and saw that it was good. He created man and man was good in His sight. The special thing about man was that man was like Him. God loves His creation, which bears His image.

Like many other relationships, there are disagreements, and there may be times where people eventually separate. The relationship between God and the man He created came to a point of separation following the man's act of disobedience, which amounted to a statement of independence, or sin. God did not stop loving man because man had sinned. However, the bond had been broken and the consequence of that was the separation of God and man. God wanted that to be restored, and restoration could only be achieved through sacrifice.

Loved

The Bible from Genesis to Revelation is the story of God's reconciliation with man. That reconciliation was planned right at the beginning; *'... he shall bruise your head, and you shall bruise his heel'* (Genesis 3:15).

God was speaking here to the serpent, and refers to the serpent's 'head' and the woman's 'seed'. The seed of the woman is Jesus, bruised by the serpent (suffering death on the cross) and ultimately crushing the head of serpent (achieving victory over Satan).

In achieving victory over Satan, Jesus ushered in reconciliation of man with God – a reconciliation hinted at right there in Genesis. It was God's plan that man should enjoy union with Him, rule over the earth and prosper in all things. We see that plan unfolding from Genesis to Revelation. We see it in Abraham's calling and the establishment of the twelve tribes of Israel, in the kings from the lineage of Judah, and in the birth of the One who is the seed of the woman.

The love that was broken was restored through the Son of God. The bride and the bridegroom's story is a fitting story because God said He had 'married' Israel and she had committed harlotry. He sent His Son to bring Israel back. Israel is now more than the geographical country, now encompasses all who live by faith in the Son of God.

The Bride of Jesus

The Jews believed that God loved the children of Israel only, but the gospel of John affirms the love of God for all people.

Revelation speaks about the marriage feast that is coming for us. The bridegroom is coming for His bride, and then there will be a wedding feast.

A wedding takes place because there is love between two people. The love story of God and His creation is expressed so well in the gospel of John, which tells us that Jesus came purely because of the love God has for us. God gave His best, His only Son. It was not a sentimental love, not a 'feeling', but an action, and one that cost Him. Christ lived and died because of the love God has for us. He healed people and raised the dead to show us that we are loved, and that there is life everlasting with God, if we so desire. The love of God has always been. It was never lost – only the living, vital, close relationship was lost.

When we understand the kind of love that God has for us, there can be no other response but to fall in love with Him.

Love is not a feeling, it is not a touch. Between a man and a woman, the relationship starts with the words, 'I love you.' Because of these three words, love is lived out and made real. People get married and spend

Loved

their lives giving expression to these words. If love was just words, there would be no need for spending time together, for understanding one another, for empathising and encouraging.

If a man says to a woman 'I love you', then hits her, swears at her, and walks away when she is in need, then those words have been scratched out and the words 'I hate you' are now inscribed. When all else has fails, love should remain.

The one who loves is the one who will remain after failure and motivate you to start again. You see couples walking in the park, holding hands, kissing and chatting, perhaps planning the future. Love is being established, but its real test comes over the long term. You can tell when two people have a deep love, and when they merely tolerate each other.

The Bible tells us that we are loved by God. He sent us Jesus so He could pay the price for our sins. He hung on the cross for us, betrayed by the ones God loves, beaten and cursed, chastised and suffered tremendously because of the object of His love. The mission of Jesus was very clear: 'Go and save my people who are perishing.' Hanging on the cross, Jesus had a choice. He could have said 'I am not the Messiah, I no longer accept this mission – it's not worth this pain.'

The Bride of Jesus

Legend has it that the Jewish people blamed Mary for making Jesus believe he was the Son of God. They said that at any time between the arrest and the crucifixion she could have saved Him by telling Him it was all a lie – He was not the Son of God, merely a man. The truth is that Jesus knew who He was, and did not need Mary to affirm it. He had all power, and could have come down, then ascended to heaven to be loved by His father rather than suffering for these people. He died for the thief who was hanging next to Him, for you and for me, and even for the soldiers who crucified Him.

He suffered because of us and the love that He has for us. Can you imagine the pain the Father experienced, looking at His Son, hearing His cries? Jesus said to the Father, 'Why have you forsaken me?' He not only felt forsaken; He was temporarily forsaken because for those moments, He bore the sins of the world upon Him, and God cannot be united with sin. The pain for Jesus was more than physical, for He was truly alone in those moments.

A father would not ordinarily give up his son for other people's sons, especially when they are ungrateful, ignorant and cruel. It could only be love.

'Love suffers long and is kind; love does not envy; love does not parade itself, is not puffed up; does not behave rudely, does not seek its own, is not provoked, thinks

no evil; does not rejoice in iniquity, but rejoices in the truth; bears all things, believes all things, hopes all things, endures all things' (1 Corinthians 13:4–7).

God is love. God is manifested in all His fullness through love. God is kind. Kindness is expressed in how we deal with a person. To show kindness to a person who is hungry, we give them food; to someone who is in pain, we comfort them. God is kind to us; when we need food or jobs we pray, 'Father help me', and He helps us because of His kindness. He takes care of us when we are sleeping, and He is there for us when we awake.

Love is patient. If God were to lose His patience towards us, we would be dead in no time. In the past hour, you and I have probably had an evil thought, a sense of anxiety, perhaps, or doubt, lust or anger ... yet God sustains us. We would not be able to survive a minute without God. He gives us countless chances. We mess up today and go back to God and He forgives us and gives us another chance to do things right. There are things that God speaks to us about and we have not listened yet – but He keeps loving us.

As a young boy, Samuel heard God's call, arose and ran to Eli, thinking Eli had called. When it happened a second time, Eli told Samuel that if he heard the voice again he should respond to God. If God were an impatient person, He would not have called a third time.

The Bride of Jesus

We are not serving a God who calls once, then moves on if we don't respond. He patiently engages with us until we hear His voice.

You can see an impatient person in a line, tapping their feet, complaining about the time it is taking to be served. A child who struggles with studies is said to be stupid by people who are impatient. At work people are impatient, wanting things done yesterday as if today does not exist. You fail once, and are labelled a failure. You undertake a business venture and it goes sour – people say you have failed. But God is different. He gives us endless chances to start again. He knows that we are dust, we are human, we are limited, and we are imperfect. His love is manifested by His patience towards us.

God wants us to love Him back, and to be patient, waiting for Him for the appointed time. Yet we are so impatient: 'God, why haven't you done this? I asked for it two months back, and I have not received it.' We judge God for not being loving enough because He has not given us what we asked at the time we expected. God says, 'Be patient, at the appointed time you will receive.'

Love does not seek its own. Jesus Christ left His majestic seat in heaven, his kingship, and came down and took the form of a human being. The One who was greater took a lower form, became lower than the angels, suffered hunger and pain, and even wept. He was not seeking His own, but seeking the good of the people, the mission of God. If He had sought His own, He might have come down and then returned and said, 'Father, these people are hopeless, they are not worthy of My life.'

Indeed, we are not worth the pain He suffered. He could have said to the Father, 'Let's start again – create a new species of human, a new Adam and Eve, and ensure that the serpent is totally destroyed or has no access to them.' Instead, He sought to restore the creation He had made.

The world is full of people who are selfish and self-centred. 'I am the one who deserves this job'; 'I must have this husband, not you'; 'My children are better than yours'; 'I have the best house.' People are seeking their own. You see it even in churches. 'These are my people, and somebody is stealing my flock.' These are the people of God, the Church of Jesus, who, in the view of some pastors, must not attend the church of their choice because that church might steal them! The universal Church of God has been assessed and stamped 'Mine!' by those created and called by God to take care of the flock.

The Church is divided because we are all seeking our own. 'His anointing is nothing compared to mine. When I just so much as look at people, they fall down.' 'I prophesy even the hidden things – even the underwear – so I am better than they are. People must come to me.'

The Bride of Jesus

'I am super-anointed.'

Your neighbour may suffer and die and you would not even know it because you are seeking your own. God is not like that. God is love. He demonstrates it by wanting the best for us all.

Christians are called to love, and not because of the personal benefit that we may gain by loving one another. Love should not be conditional.

Before salvation, an unbeliever may be spiritually held captive in a deep, dark place, and you may be tempted to think they are not worthy of being saved. Some of the people may even seem scary, but God calls them to His Kingdom.

If we would look at the love that God has for us and emulate that in our marriages, we could have the best of marriages. Show a lot of kindness to your spouse, be patient, seek the best for them.

When somebody is deeply loved, the best they can do is receive this love. It is a painful thing to love someone when they do not respond. When you love someone, you want them to love you back.

We are called to be like God. We are here on this earth to manifest God. To show the kind of love that God is.

The world needs to redefine love based on the standard of God. They can only know that standard if they see it in those who belong to God. Societal norms often measure love in monetary terms. 'He bought me a car, therefore he loves me.' 'He bought me an expensive ring, he must love me.' 'He gives me money every month ...' A woman gets excited because the man has given her money. Some people would stay in a marriage because of money. They get into relationships because of money. Some tolerate abuse because of money. Riches have a tendency to change a person's perspective about themselves. They begin to judge themselves better than others. It does not help that those who desire to be rich fall all over the rich in their quest for favours, making them demigods.

There is a poem about a woman who received flowers from the person who abused her. He did that after hurting her and she received the flowers as a peace offering and an apology. She accepted this until the last bunch of flowers which were for her funeral.

The expectation of a woman is to be loved, not abused or killed. She wants to be loved and cared for, just as the husband wants to be loved and cared for. The bride of Jesus is called into a relationship based on love. She is loved and must love as well.

The Church is called to reveal the love of God. *'But whoever keeps His word, truly the love of God is perfected*

The Bride of Jesus

in him. By this we know that we are in Him' (1 John 2:5).

The husband is called to love his wife. Jesus has already proven His love, hanging on the cross for His bride, paying the price for the sins of many.

'By this we know love, because He laid down His life for us. And we also ought to lay down our lives for the brethren' (1 John 3:16).

'Beloved, let us love one another, for love is of God; and everyone who loves is born of God and knows God' (1 John 4:7).

15
Mature

> 'And He Himself gave some to be apostles, some prophets, some evangelists, and some pastors and teachers, for the equipping of the saints for the work of ministry ... that we should no longer be children, tossed to and fro and carried about with every wind of doctrine, by the trickery of men, in the cunning craftiness of deceitful plotting'
>
> (Ephesians 4:11, 14).

Growing up, I was taught many things by my mother. She made sure I knew how to cook, clean the house and take care of myself. Parenting is preparing a child for adulthood. Society may be turning against the idea of a woman having a particular domestic role, but I must say, training in the basics goes a long way when you get married.

The Bride of Jesus

We may protest against domesticating girls, yet many of us find pleasure in cooking a great meal and seeing our husband enjoy it. I speak as someone who had both homemaking and the making of a career demonstrated. My mother exemplified both domestication and professionalism. She became a wife, a mother to four children, and then went back to high school and college, which she completed in her thirties. She then became a teacher.

Looking back, I realise how I hated house chores, but I did them. She wanted the pots shining so she could see them from afar when she came home. She wanted the floor shining brightly – thank God for ceramic tiles. She also taught me personal grooming. When I grew up and got married, I was ready to take on the role of wife. I was never a housewife, and I still don't like domestic chores, but I am prepared to do them. My house must be clean, the food must be wholesome and I must be well presented – this is what I was taught.

When my younger sister grew up, she was the last born and spoilt. She was not taught much as I was, but sat on laps and played princess. Then she came to stay in my home, where I taught her domestic chores. We fought tooth and nail, but in the end, my pots had to shine as my mother's had. As stubborn as she was, she is grateful that she had an equally stubborn sister. She learned.

Mature

Now she is a wife and mother, and can take care of her home properly.

My husband is one of that rare breed – a very clean and neat man. If I had not been prepared, we would have fought way too much. I would be frustrated with him, and he with me. Dishes never stay in the sink overnight – that is his standard and mine, as it was my mother's when I was a girl. She prepared me to be the wife and mother that I am today, teaching me everything that I now practise. My time with her, in other words, was preparation time, enabling me to mature.

In some cultures, boys go to the mountain for circumcision and spend time there being taught how to be a man. Some churches have youth services where young girls and boys are taught about issues that pertain to young people in a tough world, so that they grow and become mature, losing immature ideas.

The bride of Jesus has been provided with tutors and mentors in the form of apostles, evangelists, prophets, teachers and preachers. These are charged with equipping the saints for the work of ministry. That statement is important. The Church is not being prepared for the coming of Christ, but for the work of ministry. Christ's coming was already taken care of when we were saved – it is a given. What is left after salvation is for the believer to be equipped for the work of ministry. Ministry work

The Bride of Jesus

was never meant for the ministers, but for the saints! Ministers are charged with preparing saints to go out and minister. The Gospel was not meant to be preached by the preachers and evangelists only, but by the saints – everyone who believes.

'How then shall they call on Him in whom they have not believed? And how shall they believe in Him of whom they have not heard? And how shall they hear without a preacher? And how shall they preach unless they are sent? As it is written: "How beautiful are the feet of those who preach the gospel of peace, who bring glad tidings of good things!" (Romans 10:14-15).

Every meeting of the saints is an opportunity for equipping the bride of Jesus. She must be ready to go out there and speak about her bridegroom, spread the Good News about the Messiah. She must be the light that shines in the darkness. She must be the light that attracts people to come to the light and be saved. She must be the salt that makes food edible. She can be that only when she is taught.

When a woman gets married, she cannot continually go back home to be taught. She cannot bring her mother to take care of her responsibilities in the home. New brides make mistakes, mess up the food, and may even struggle to cope with the demands of marriage. A prepared bride is able to adjust soon enough.

Mature

Jesus took three and half years teaching the disciples about the kingdom of God. He also spent time answering their questions on issues when they needed clarity. He was able to explain parables to them – explanations that others never heard. They were privileged to be taught by the Master. They also witnessed the work Jesus did.

When He opened the eyes of a man born blind, something that had never been done before, the disciples were there to witness it. When He healed the man lame for 38 years, the woman oppressed for 18 years and the woman bleeding for 12 years, they were there to witness that infirmities that had been around for a long time would bow to Jesus. They saw Jesus multiply a few fish and loaves of bread. They were there to see Him raise Lazarus who had been dead four days – the ultimate miracle.

The disciples were matured over time, and when Christ left, they were ready to do as He did. They healed the lame man at the gate called Beautiful. They now knew that it was possible to heal a person who had been living with a disability since birth. It was not a big deal for them to exorcise Simon the sorcerer, as they had seen Jesus dealing with far stronger demons in the men of Gadarene. They would not back down from a challenge because they were confident in the Lord and His power.

The Bride of Jesus

The Church today faces sickness as in Bible times. Despite increases in our lifespan due to improved medical care, people still die from incurable diseases. Cancer, HIV/Aids, diabetes, high blood pressure, strokes and many more diseases kill people daily. Many false pastors and prophets have arisen to take advantage of the desperation of the sick. They charge exorbitant fees to pray for a sick person. People have come to a point where they believe that unless they get prayed for by a specific 'man of God', they will not be healed.

The Church is not being prepared and equipped to heal the sick as a work of ministry. When sick and oppressed people come to the altar, many sit in judgment of them, seeking the cause of the affliction instead of casting the demon out. When the disciples asked; *'Rabbi, who sinned, this man or his parents, that he was born blind?'* (John 9:2), Jesus responded *'Neither this man nor his parents sinned, but that the works of God should be revealed in him'* (John 9:3). So it had nothing to do with sin, it was an opportunity for God to do a miracle. Instead of being judgmental, the church should seek the face of God to bring deliverance.

People of God are afraid to cast demons out, just in case they jump out of the person and enter them! What a sorry state of affairs. The apostles were not afraid of demons. Even when there was one they could not cast out,

Mature

they went ahead and tried – they failed trying.

People come to church every Sunday and go home without having hands laid on them. Church has become like a trip to the doctor, where you receive a prescription for your exclusive use only, to last only seven days – then you must go back, and have your prescription filled. People are not being prepared to lay hands on their sick children at home, or to cast out demons in daily life.

I remember an episode in church where a demon was being cast out, and the person said, 'Father, we do not want to fellowship with devils here.' I was shocked. What devil would leave when it hears such a prayer? He said cast them out, not complain about them to Me! I have heard people shouting from the pews, 'That's a devil!' but they sit and do nothing about it. Jesus did not say identify the demon, He said cast it out. If you see a demon, then you must use the power Christ has given you to cast it out, or say nothing.

I have also seen a very old woman getting up and walking slowly to the prayer line, while the ushers ran towards her, urging her to sit down in front for prayer; she walked right past them, and approached a girl who was screaming. She then pointed her finger at the demon and cast it out. The girl fell down, and the woman walked slowly back to her seat.

The Bride of Jesus

That is the bride of Jesus! She does not sit and talk badly about her little sister in the Lord – she delivers her from bondage, the affliction of the devil. She does not complain about the time wasted in praying for the afflicted; she rises up and deals with the issue – and then we all go home early.

The Bible tells us that when the girl with the spirit of divination followed Paul around, he was irritated by the spirit. He cast it out. He did not tell the people to keep the girl quiet. He did not tell them to send her to the back room. He just cast the devil out. If the Church were to rise up in unity against the evil spirits in the Church, then their removal would be swift, and then we won't complain about time. One can chase a thousand, two can chase ten thousand. The church with only fifty people can chase millions.

Is the Church equipped? Is the Church maturing? The Church has become like a young bride who encounters a hungry husband and has no clue how to cook. She begins to call her mother and ask for recipes. The mother is far and the advice she gives results in food in the bin. She should have been prepared.

Jesus spent time teaching the disciples, equipping them with knowledge, preparing them for ministry. When they could not cast a demon out, He told them that, that kind did not come out except by prayer. Some versions add 'and fasting'. They had to know that there were stubborn spirits that would need effort in prayer to cast out. Jesus had been in prayer all night when He found the disciples trying and failing to cast out a demon. They would not always have Jesus in the flesh with them. They needed to grow up, put on some spiritual muscles, and deal with the enemy. Jesus showed them that there is no demon that cannot be cast out.

Later, apostles went out to teach the growing Church. When they found that administration was taking a lot of their time, they appointed men to deal with it so that they could focus on teaching and prayer. Paul's prayer was always that the brethren would grow in knowledge. To the church in Colossae, he wrote: *'For this reason we also, since the day we heard it, do not cease to pray for you, and to ask that you may be filled with the knowledge of His will in all wisdom and spiritual understanding; that you may walk worthy of the Lord, fully pleasing Him, being fruitful in every good work and increasing in the knowledge of God; strengthened with all might, according to His glorious power, for all patience and longsuffering with joy; giving thanks to the Father who has qualified us to be partakers of the inheritance of the saints in the light'* (Colossians 1:9–11).

Wisdom is needed to do what is right before God. Spiritual understanding brings clarity on things unseen and things that cannot be understood in the flesh. When divisions arose in the Church, some saying they were of Paul, others of Apollos, the situation required wisdom and spiritual understanding, so that the congregation would lift up the name of Jesus.

It has become the norm today for servants of God to claim people for themselves, simply because they led them to Christ. The people of God have become the people of the servants of God. Neither Paul, nor Apollos, nor Peter had any right to the people of God. Wisdom walks away from such fights, after rebuking people for dividing the church.

Social media is good for spreading the Good News, but it is also used for spreading divisions within the body of Christ. Spiritual understanding is critical if we are to discern what is behind a post on social media. Fake news is issued daily, mocking the Church, and too many believers fall for it without checking on its source. Some posts are not fake, but simply personal opinions that get us all worked up and ready to fight over nothing.

The unbelievers look and shake their heads, seeing nothing attractive in the behavior of the children of God. It takes maturity to walk away. I had one 'fight' on social media regarding a post I made. I remained in the argument for longer than necessary. I remember a friend joking with me the following day that it must have been Boxing Day the previous day. That argument ended when the Holy Spirit rebuked me – I still had counter arguments up my sleeve, but it was not necessary to express them. Some get a kick out of mocking believers, especially pastors and especially female pastors. Maturity, wisdom and the Holy Spirit cause us to walk away from such empty mockery. We always have the option to 'delete' and move on.

'Therefore, when the Lord knew that the Pharisees had heard that Jesus made and baptized more disciples than John (though Jesus Himself did not baptize, but His disciples), He left Judea and departed again to Galilee' (John 4:1–2). Jesus would not steal the limelight from John the Baptist.

He was secured in His role as the Messiah. John the Baptist had his role to fulfill. When you look down on another servant, you are saying God made the wrong choice. Leave that servant of God to do what they are called to do, no matter how small and insignificant in your opinion.

I can imagine how much fuel might be added to the pride of an immature believer when he is told that he is healing more people, has more members, and prophesies more accurately than another servant of God. It becomes headline news: 'Look what I did!' – as if the work of God is an achievement for an individual. Jesus said,

The Bride of Jesus

'... *for without Me you can do nothing*' (John 15:5). In addition, Jesus said of Himself, '*The Son can do nothing of Himself, but what He sees the Father do*' (John 5:19). Yet a human being boasts about what he has achieved as if by his own power. Maturity will bring you to a point of magnifying He who holds the power – only Jesus.

We need to be cautious on social media. Some posts are captured by others; when you grow up and become successful, they draw out that file and attack you with it. A wise bride knows not to air her dirty linen in public. She knows her corner, her one safe person to whom she can pour out her heart. She knows better than to come across as a street fighter. Imagine a husband that is always having to extricate his wife from street fights – what an embarrassment, to say the least.

The maturity of the disciples went beyond believing for things and miracles. Their characters changed. Peter, an abrasive and impulsive man who was always ready to fight, and who denied Jesus three times, underwent a process of maturing. He changed.

When he preached on the Day of Pentecost, he was not afraid. The people who had crucified Jesus were still in Jerusalem. The same Peter who denied Jesus in fear and trembling stood up and accused them of killing Jesus. Fear was gone. His time with Jesus had prepared him to stand up and proclaim Jesus resurrected.

Mature

'Now when they saw the boldness of Peter and John, and perceived that they were uneducated and untrained men, they marveled. And they realized that they had been with Jesus' (Acts 4:13).

Peter allowed himself to mature and change. He spoke with boldness and wisdom, to the point that people marveled, and ascribed his wisdom to the fact that he had been with Jesus. Can people ascribe your behavior to Jesus? When you fight your brethren, who taught you to behave that way?

Once at the office, a co-worker fell sick. I was called to come and pray for her. She was in a bad state and experiencing terrible pain. As I was praying, others were in a commotion, some calling for an ambulance. I called for the other believers I knew to come and join me in prayer. As the pain subsided and the woman composed herself, some said she should still go to hospital. They were speaking contrary to what she stated and believed – that she was fine. Later she checked in with a doctor, took a few days off, and was completely well.

The battle is out there. The enemy attacks in many ways, and believers need to be mature and ready at any time to minister. Let it be known that there is someone in your office who can pray for the sick. Unless the bride of Jesus is mature and ready, she will run away every time the devil rears his ugly head.

The Bride of Jesus

The Church faces inner stresses, just as the early Church did. Where there are two people, there are bound to be disagreements. No two people ever thought the same and agreed on everything. A mature person knows how to deal with these expected disagreements.

When Paul saw Peter behaving like a hypocrite in front of the Jews, he did not go around telling people how Peter acted differently when he was with Jews than when away from the Jews. No. He went straight to Peter and confronted him, brother to brother. Similarly, we too, should settle the matter with the one who has offended us; we may call a third person if necessary, but there is never any justification to discuss our offences widely.

When the issue of circumcision arose, the apostles met in Jerusalem to take counsel on the matter. In discussions, each was given an opportunity to present his views and understanding. The council came up with a decision and they sent certain brothers to the churches to convey the message.

Today, when there is a disagreement, it lands first on social media, long before the person who is allegedly in the wrong knows of it. The world is told so that they avoid the brother who has supposedly done something wrong. The rest of the flock is judged on whether they 'like' the message of the accuser. The mistake of the brother is apparently beyond forgiveness. If he is a teacher or pastor, the very message of God that he brings will not be accepted because of some doctrinal error he may have made.

A mature bride talks first to her husband about an issue she is not happy with. If the matter is not resolved, she may speak to her in-laws or the spiritual authority in her life. A mature bride does not go around telling other people how bad her husband is. She seeks to bring peace to her household.

The Church has to rise to a greater level of maturity in every respect. The Church has a bigger enemy than the brethren within it. The enemy that brings strife in the Church has to be dealt with.

Unless the Church is prepared for battle, the enemy will continuously have free reign and disrupt the Word of God from going out. Unless the Church is prepared to cast out the demon of division from its midst, that demon will continue to afflict the people of God. Unless the Church realises the potent power that is within, given on the Day of Pentecost, she will continue to be subject to the wiles of the devil and never live the reality that the Lord has triumphed over the devil on the cross.

The Church is tossed to and fro by doctrinal winds these days. Matters that do not determine salvation are breaking the body of Christ apart. It is as if one is saying, 'I am of Apollos' and another is saying 'I am of Paul'.

The Bride of Jesus

Are any of these leaders Jesus? The tithe is a matter over which we love to bicker. In the early Church there was never a debate about the tithe; the book of Acts, which is a record of the unfolding Church after the departure of the Lord, shows that the people gave their all, and willingly. Yet giving a tenth is a big debate these days, each group belittling the other for their stance on the topic. The wind is blowing and the Church is tossed to and fro. Search the Scriptures, Jesus said. The mature Church searches the Scripture to see if what is said is true.

While the Church bickers over issues that do not affect salvation, unbelievers look and walk past. 'No thanks,' they say. The Church is at times like a contentious woman in Proverbs; her husband would rather sleep on the roof top than with such a woman.

The message of the Good News is simple, and as valid as ever. That message, fully grasped, is powerful enough to get the Church running again in victory.

Jesus is coming soon. He wants to find a mature bride. He wants to find a bride who has the home front taken care of. He wants to find the home swept clean and full of the Word. He wants to find the children cleaned up and nourished by the Word. He wants to find the children growing and maturing. He wants a church that stands her ground.

Mature

Maybe the charge should be against the caretakers of the Church. What report will the Lord get from those He entrusted to equip His bride and bring her to maturity? Can the apostles, prophets, evangelists, teachers and preachers stand with boldness and say, 'We have equipped your bride, Lord. She is ready, she has long been ready?' Jesus will surely want an account. He did not charge His servants with keeping His bride a baby. He wants her to grow and mature.

The Church has to move from the elementary issues, as babies outgrow milk. Elementary arguments about tithing and baptisms must come to an end. Let the Church begin to influence the market place, parliament, the offices, the boardrooms, the factories. How wonderful a sound it would be to find workers working and singing, 'Holy, holy, holy are you Lord!'

16
Grounded in the Word

'Therefore, my beloved brethren, be steadfast, immovable, always abounding in the work of the Lord, knowing that your labor is not in vain in the Lord'

(1 Corinthians 15:58).

A story is told of a woman who was always quick to pack her bags and leave after an argument with her husband. She would return to her parents and wait for him to come begging for her to come home.

She did that many times until one day, while she was packing after an argument, he did not beg her to stay as before, but started assisting her. He asked her if she had everything she needed. He helped her locate the items she wanted, then conveyed her bags to the car. She was shocked.

The Bride of Jesus

How could he help her pack? In fact he was ensuring that she had everything she owned, so that she could leave for good.

This is a story that many in the Church are living. The suitcases are worn out not because people are touring the world, but because they go back and forth. It is such a tiring exercise.

Personally, I don't mind packing, but unpacking is a chore I could do without. I travel on business a lot and when I come home, I bless God for my daughter who unpacks my bags for me. I don't have the experience of packing to leave after an argument, then packing to come back home again. Not that we don't have occasional arguments at home. But packing to leave has never been an option for me.

I must hasten to add that there are women who pack and leave justifiably. Their mistake may well be in returning. Life is too precious to be beaten and abused by a man, and to go back and forth under such circumstances is usually ill advised.

Marriage is meant to be until death. It is not meant to be a yoyo, both partners going up and down, back and forth. It is a lifetime commitment of two people who promise to remain together.

The enemy is always against what God has ordained. He is guilty of separating man from God in the beginning. He is guilty of causing strife between Adam and Eve. After their deception, Adam forgot that she was *'bone of my bones, and flesh of my flesh'* (Genesis 2:23).

She became *'the woman whom You gave to be with me, she gave me of the tree, and I ate'* (Genesis 3:12). The enemy has been causing strife and divisions ever since, in marriages, homes and workplaces, and even in the Church.

What the enemy did was to cause Eve to doubt what God had said and to entertain a different view of the instructions of God. She began to think there was more to that tree than what God had told Adam. Her view of God shifted from God as provider to God as withholder of the truth; a God who did not want them to know good and evil, or to be like Him.

Satan is doing the same in marriages. Two people marry because they love one another. All of a sudden, she is no longer sufficient – he wants more, and looks for it outside of the marriage. She is no longer fun to be with. She is no longer slim enough or beautiful enough. Since he no longer pays attention to her or gives her money, she looks elsewhere, too.

The Bride of Jesus

Eventually things deteriorate so far that he hardly comes home, the marriage barely exists, and she packs her bags and leaves.

Things and people change over time, and we need to accept this in our marriages. The issue is how we respond to change. The economy may nosedive, household finances may become tight, but that does not change the fact that your husband loves you and chose you.

He may be emotionally affected by the change in financial status, so that he becomes anxious or short tempered. These kinds of changes require that a woman faces the world armed with the Word of God, rather than with an empty suitcase, just waiting to be filled at the first sign of trouble.

Circumstances changed for the widow in the Old Testament who was hounded by her husband's creditors. The husband who shielded her was no longer there to fulfil his responsibilities. The creditors demanded her sons, her only hope of sustenance. Instead of running away from her circumstances, she went to the servant of God, Elisha, pleading her case with him, and her problem was solved. Her solution was not to run away from the problem, but to seek the intervention of God.

For Naomi, circumstances changed twice. Famine in Bethlehem caused her husband to take the family to the country of Moab. This was a new country and culture, and being there must have involved great personal adjustment on her part. After many years her husband died in the foreign land, and Naomi had nothing, so she returned to her home town of Bethlehem. She was faithful and remained with him to the end, only returning to her home country after he passed on. Marriage should not end because the finances have dried up. Solutions must be found.

Sarah had a similar experience. She followed her husband to the Promised Land, on the understanding that it was a land of milk and honey. As soon as they arrived, famine struck the land. I can imagine the woman looking at her husband and the dry fields and saying, 'Where is the milk and honey God promised you, Abraham?' Abraham then took her to Egypt, where he asked her to pretend to be his sister. Pharaoh saw her and wanted her as his wife, but God saved her from that situation.

Later, in the land of Gerar, Abimelech took Sarah as his wife. God saved her again. I wonder, what manner of woman was this? She stuck by her husband no matter what. Sarah was grounded in her faith and held on to the promises of God. She was not tossed to and fro by the winds of trouble.

'By faith Sarah herself also received strength to conceive seed, and she bore a child when she was past the

The Bride of Jesus

age, because she judged Him faithful who had promised' (Hebrews 11:11).

God showed Himself faithful to the widow, Naomi and Sarah, and He surely has not changed now. He is available to help couples today, who know His faithfulness and who strive to remain faithful to His Word.

The fact that two people love each other does not make them immune to attacks. Within the family, attacks may come in the form of accusations and poor treatment. Young brides loath an oppressive mother-in-law and sisters-in-law. Husbands are tested and weighed up by their in-laws, and looked down upon if they do not measure up. Attacks may come from outside, with people bringing accusations. Temptations will also attack the marriage, and yielding to them has caused many breakups.

Some marriages are affected by outsiders' behaviour and opinions. Women tend to observe what other husbands do and compare their behaviour to their own husband. Ever heard a woman say, 'Mr So-and so opens the door of the car for his wife – why don't you do the same for me?' Poor husband now has to strive to be like someone his wife tells him about. Truly, we put unnecessary pressure on our husbands to buy us big homes and cars not because we need them, but because of our friends.

Grounded in the Word

It is not wrong to desire good things in life, but other people's standards of living should not be imposed on our budget. Be realistic.

Societal norms and cultures change over generations. There are things that were unheard of in times past, but are now acceptable as the norm, and are no longer the exception. What are we to do?

Be grounded as a person. You cannot chase the Joneses – they have their own source of income. You cannot change God's standard because of society. The bride of Jesus is expected to obey the Word of God in whatever generation she lives, in whatever circumstances she finds herself and whatever the behaviour and opinions of others may be.

The Word of God is eternally true and is the standard for the believer. Time should not make your ground shift. If God said it, and you believe it, then stand on that Word. Abraham believed God and it was credited to him as righteousness.

A full 24 years passed before the son God promised to him was born. During that time, doubt came to visit, and Abraham had a child with Hagar. That did not stop God from releasing the son He had promised at the appointed time. If Abraham had remained grounded in the Word of God and kept his faith strong, there would not

The Bride of Jesus

have been an Ishmael, and possibly no war in the Middle East today. Yet even now, God is faithful, and blesses both the children of Ishmael and Isaac.

God told Abraham that his sons would be slaves in a foreign land for more than 400 years and that at the appointed time, He would take them out of that land. Try blocking the fulfilment of the Word of God – like Pharaoh, you will lose much. The time they spent as slaves was long, but the Word of God was already spoken, and when it was time, nothing could stop them from leaving Egypt.

The bride of Jesus is called to a standing position, grounded and unmoved. *'Therefore, since we are receiving a kingdom which cannot be shaken, let us have grace, by which we may serve God acceptably with reverence and godly fear. For our God is a consuming fire'* (Hebrews 12:28).

We are too easily moved by changes in circumstances, and lose out on much of our blessings because we shift and falter, leave and return, and cannot stick to the promises we make. The Bible shows that God's plan is never shaken. Believers need to develop patience and character, and wait awhile in Egypt when required. Our reward will come.

Grounded in the Word

I recently obtained access to a national, well-established retailer for the books I publish. There was a four-year process of being denied access over and over again. Every time I asked, I was referred to other distributors. When I approached them, some did not like my books – which is to be expected of secular distributors. I would go back to the original retailer and they would send me the same list of referrals. It was an effort to get there, but I did not give up. Companies would not respond to emails, nor even answer their phones.

Four years after I began the process, I sent an email to the company again. Same response – 'Here is a list of other companies you may try'. I took a deep breath and closed the email. A few days later, God prompted me to re-open the email and respond to it. I prayed before writing. Then I put my case to them. I was not just selling my own books, but those of many other writers. If I struggled to gain access to them with my few books, how much more would others struggle who had only one book? I received a response the same day – my application was approved.

I used the time when I struggled to get access to grow as a writer. They want good quality books and that takes time and hard work.

Had I given up, I would not have known the faithfulness of God in answering prayer. I must say, that four

The Bride of Jesus

years felt like a long time. Yet still, I am grateful for the opportunity. One of the fruits of the Spirit is patience. Our problem is not that God does not answer our prayers, but that we lack the patience and the willingness to persist. Don't give up at the first sign of opposition.

Jesus is coming for a bride who knows how to deal with opposition: *'Finally, my brethren, be strong in the Lord and in the power of His might. Put on the whole armor of God, that you may be able to stand against the wiles of the devil ... Therefore take up the whole armor of God, that you may be able to withstand in the evil day, and having done all, to stand'* (Ephesians 6:10–11, 13).

Be strong in the Lord, this scripture says. Do not be shaken. The battle is not with a person whom you see and can fight with physically. The battle is spiritual and requires spiritual armour which can defeat the enemy who cannot be seen. The wiles of the devil cannot be defeated by packing your bags and leaving the Church, your home or your business. The devil is defeated by using the armour of God. The Kingdom of God cannot be shaken, and neither should its citizens.

You cannot be a believer and then pack your bags and leave your church because the enemy has used your sister in the Lord to gossip about you. That is a big 'No'. You cannot leave because the brother who asked you to marry him has found someone else and dumped you. That

Grounded in the Word

is another big no. You did not come to church to be married by the brother, but to worship God and fellowship with the brethren. People are talking about the incident – so what? They must have spoken about the poor widow, Naomi and barren Sarah – and even the great prophet Elijah who, after calling down fire from heaven, ran to a cave, tired and worn out.

We need to stop being tossed about by the behaviour of others and by false Bible interpretations that suit societal norms and standards. If the Bible calls drunkenness sin, the fact that a pastor got drunk yesterday does not make it less of a sin. The fact that governments have legalised some things contrary to the Word of God does not mean the Church should shift and align with the government. We are called to submit to authority, the first authority being God. The rest can line up after God.

The Church is divided on the issue of the work of the Holy Spirit. Some say tongues are wrong, prophecies are false. The question is, what does the Bible say concerning these things? Do we tell God that since there are false prophets here, as He warned us there would be, we reject all prophecies? Who stands to benefit most if the Church is no longer empowered by praying to God in the heavenly language? Who rejoices when the voice of God is silenced in the Church because we are offended by a few false prophets? Did God not say they would come? Why is the Church now shaken by these things to the point of running in the opposite direction to the Word of God?

Instead of praying for the true prophets to arise, many would rather that all prophets disappear. Such fearful believers would rather we go back to the time in Israel where *'... the word of the* L*ORD* *was rare in those days; there was no widespread revelation'* (1 Samuel 3:1). What will the believers have if they reject the power and work of the Holy Ghost because of a few false prophets?

'I marvel that you are turning away so soon from Him who called you in the grace of Christ, to a different gospel, which is not another; but there are some who trouble you and want to pervert the gospel of Christ' (Galatians 1:6–7). We cannot afford to move away from this Gospel because of these people. This Gospel is the power of God for us who believe.

The church in Galatia experienced a crisis when some perverted the Gospel, wanting to keep the believers in bondage. Paul's response was that even if angels were to preach such a false gospel, let them be accursed. Instead of being grounded in the Word of God, believers find themselves grounded in the words of man. On the one side we have believers abandoning the Word of God by running after false prophets, and on the other hand we have believers abandoning the Word of God by dismissing all prophecy as false and all prophets as charlatans. But the Word of God stands true and unmoved.

'And this occurred because of false brethren secretly brought in (who came in by stealth to spy out our liberty which we have in Christ Jesus, that they might bring us into bondage), to whom we did not yield submission even for an hour, that the truth of the gospel might continue with you' (Galatians 2:4–5).

The bride of Jesus is strengthened by the brethren, her robe washed in the blood of Jesus, her spirit empowered by the Holy Spirit and her character formed by the Word. As a result, she is victorious in every area. Be grounded and remain steadfast in the word of God, no matter what the circumstances.

17
Positioned to influence

'So he called ten of his servants, delivered to them ten minas, and said to them, 'Do business till I come' (Luke 19:13).

The bride of Jesus is not called to be in the kitchen barefoot and pregnant as may have been the case in ancient times. Praise God, she can be pregnant in the office and serve God right there. She is like the Proverbs 31 woman who is virtuous, resourceful, hardworking and successful – not one or the other.

In the olden days, women who stayed at home found things to do and called them hobbies. After the house was cleaned, clothes were washed and children fed, there may have been time to knit or sew a few items and sell to friends and the community. Some baked and made a little money. These days, stay-at-home wives use the internet to make money. So the business of being a wife is taken care of, as is the business of making money and serving the community. This chapter is not about money, but about influencing society with our God-given talents.

I read a book about a doctor whose son had cancer. As a medical professional, he sought medical help until there was nothing medical science could do. Then he sought the Lord's intervention to heal his son. In his desperation, he stopped working as a medical professional and embarked on a spiritual journey. He thought the Lord was calling him to missions, but the Lord told him to go back to the hospital and do what he had been called to do; his ministry was right there. There were souls in that hospital who needed to see and hear from God.

He began to perform miracles in that hospital. The very first was to raise a dead man back to life. A man had died during a heart operation, and both this doctor and his colleagues had left the room after certifying the man dead. The doctor came back into the room while the nurse was preparing the body, and started to pray in tongues for the first time, calling on God to raise him up. The man arose, and the doctor went on to heal many people through prayer. In his book, he tells of a man whose leg was due to be amputated a week later because of an ulcer that would not heal. The afflicted man was in the doctor's rooms for his wife's appointment, when the doc-

Positioned to influence

tor noticed the leg and asked about it. When he heard that it was due to be amputated, he offered him prayer and asked him to come back the following week, before the date of the amputation. The man returned as agreed, pulled up his trousers and asked the doctor to identify which leg had had the ulcer. Glory to Jesus, the doctor could not even tell which of the legs it was – they were both smooth and healthy.

This is the power of God at work in the workplace. The mission of God is not always in the pulpit, but in the office, on the factory floor, on the highways and byways, in the school yard and in parliament. This doctor was called to serve God in the theatre room, in the hospital ward, in his office. He was called to bring God to his fellow medical professionals who had to know that God is alive and powerful.

Jesus gave this parable:

'A certain nobleman went into a far country to receive for himself a kingdom and to return. So he called ten of his servants, delivered to them ten minas, and said to them, "Do business till I come." And so it was that when he returned, having received the kingdom, he then commanded these servants, to whom he had given the money, to be called to him, that he might know how much every man had gained by trading. Then came the first, saying, "Master, your mina has earned ten minas." And he said to

The Bride of Jesus

him, "Well done, good servant; because you were faithful in a very little, have authority over ten cities." And the second came, saying, "Master, your mina has earned five minas." Likewise he said to him, "You also be over five cities." Then another came, saying, "Master, here is your mina, which I have kept put away in a handkerchief. For I feared you, because you are an austere man. You collect what you did not deposit, and reap what you did not sow." And he said to him, "Out of your own mouth I will judge you, you wicked servant. You knew that I was an austere man, collecting what I did not deposit and reaping what I did not sow. Why then did you not put my money in the bank, that at my coming I might have collected it with interest?" And he said to those who stood by, "Take the mina from him, and give it to him who has ten minas." For I say to you, that to everyone who has will be given; and from him who does not have, even what he has will be taken away from him' (Luke 19:12

In the above parable, Jesus confirms that there will be a time lapse between His ascension and His return. Jesus wanted His followers to understand that while He was gone, life had to go on and they had to work. The men in the parable were given different amounts of money, which represent the various different gifts that each person has. Some may seem to have more gifts, but collectively they all work for the good of everyone. Some people use their gifts for good, while others claim a calling and neglect their natural gifts. This parable is clear that the fruitful ones did not have only one talent or gift, but many.

We need to influence the market place with our gifts. The ten minas were given to the servants, and they were expected to use them for profit. Two did exactly that, while the foolish servant failed to do so. The master expects us to use our minas, or natural talents. Being called does not mean your talents are to be buried. Do business until the Lord comes. This is as applicable to the one called to the pulpit as it is to the one called to serve in other ways. We all have different skills, abilities and talents; some are good at one or two things, and some excel at many. We should not neglect any of the gifts we have.

Today, many servants of God are using all their talents, both in the pulpit and in the secular world. Those who have fewer talents often point fingers and accuse such ministers of greed, unable to accept that they possess talents in more than one area. Poverty is nobody's friend. The righteous never beg for bread, they are never forsaken. Paul, the apostle of Jesus whose work forms a big part of the New Testament, worked diligently for the Lord. He was a tentmaker, earning money so that he would not be a burden to anyone. He did not wait for hand-outs or use guilt to make people bring tithes and

The Bride of Jesus

offerings so that he could eat.

He may have received offerings when they were given freely, but he also used his hands to make enough money for his own upkeep. *'And he found a certain Jew named Aquila, born in Pontus, who had recently come from Italy with his wife Priscilla (because Claudius had commanded all the Jews to depart from Rome); and he came to them. So, because he was of the same trade, he stayed with them and worked; for by occupation they were tentmakers. And he reasoned in the synagogue every Sabbath, and persuaded both Jews and Greeks. So Paul still remained a good while. Then he took leave of the brethren and sailed for Syria, and Priscilla and Aquila were with him. He had his hair cut off at Cenchrea, for he had taken a vow."* (Acts 18:2)

Paul did not depend on his hosts Priscilla and Aquila. He worked for his upkeep. He was an apostle, admired by the believers, yet he did not use his position to abuse their kindness. Paul used his talents and his spiritual gifts. His calling was not a ticket for becoming rich. His own talent would make him rich if he wished it to. He was doing business until Jesus came or he went to Jesus.

Luke, a medical doctor, travelled with Paul and witnessed his ministry. He was qualified to examine the sick as they travelled, even though Paul might have preferred that the sick be healed by the Holy Spirit. During

Positioned to influence

missionary work, there will always be someone needing medical attention. Luke's profession would have brought people needing help to him, and he could have used such opportunities to preach the Good News to them.

Peter, Andrew, James and John were fishermen. They put their work on hold when they went ministering with Jesus, but from time to time would find themselves fishing again. Jesus found them fishing after His resurrection. Jesus used Peter's profession to get the tax money, when he sent him to seek out a fish. When he preached, Jesus used the boat belonging to Peter and his family. We are called to fund Kingdom business with our talents.

We are also called to raise up the banner of righteousness. John the Baptist was a lone voice speaking against the immoral rulers of his time. He did not just preach about the coming Messiah, put raised up the moral compass for everyone to see. Christians in parliament are doing God a disservice when they take care of their purses and keep quiet about the moral issues. Your voice alone may not bring change, but it will sound out for years to come, long after you are gone. We do not know how many people changed because of John the Baptist, but we still talk about him today.

In the temple courts, a highly educated man called Nicodemus heard and saw the miracles that Jesus was doing. His conscience was pricked. One night he came to Jesus secretly so that he could question Him more closely and investigate the matter of salvation. The salvation of certain people in high places may well depend on a few bold Christians who take the stage and speak up about Jesus.

There was also the young maidservant in the house of Naaman. When her master was sick, she told him that there was a prophet who could help him. She could have just minded her own business, but she had an opportunity to reveal God to this man. Naaman went to see Elisha and was healed. So strong was his conviction that his conscience was troubled about what he was doing back home: *'Then, if not, please let your servant be given two mule-loads of earth; for your servant will no longer offer either burnt offering or sacrifice to other gods, but to the* LORD. *Yet in this thing may the Lord pardon your servant: when my master goes into the temple of Rimmon to worship there, and he leans on my hand, and I bow down in the temple of Rimmon—when I bow down in the temple of Rimmon, may the* LORD *please pardon your servant in this thing'* (2 Kings 5:17–18).

It is a great pity that some servants of God, when given the podium to speak, fail to mention their faith or the work of God in their lives. They would rather sing the praises of fellow politicians, following the lead of others,

Positioned to influence

than speak about Jesus right there and then – in their workplace.

Never underestimate the impact of speaking out for the kingdom of God. Some people only get to know the power of God when a believer stands their ground and declares God to be God. Take the Hebrew boys in the book of Daniel. They had a choice; they could blend in or they could remain steadfast in their faith, and they chose the latter. After being thrown into the fiery furnace, their faith and the results of their faith brought the king to his knees in acknowledgment of God.

'Nebuchadnezzar spoke, saying, "Blessed be the God of Shadrach, Meshach, and Abed-Nego, who sent His Angel and delivered His servants who trusted in Him, and they have frustrated the king's word, and yielded their bodies, that they should not serve nor worship any god except their own God! Therefore I make a decree that any people, nation, or language which speaks anything amiss against the God of Shadrach, Meshach, and Abed-Nego shall be cut in pieces, and their houses shall be made an ash heap; because there is no other God who can deliver like this"' (Daniel 3:28–29).

How will the unbelievers know God unless the believers testify about Him, not just in preaching but in standing their ground? The bride of Jesus is called to stand for the truth and defend this Gospel and her faith.

The Bride of Jesus

As a bride, it is my duty to defend my husband. My mother taught me very well. One can never speak badly about my father in her presence, or about us, her children. A wife defends her family. A wife presents her family in a positive light. It is a sign of immaturity for a woman to go around bad-mouthing her husband. After all is said and done, you still go back to your husband and the people are left with a negative picture of both you and your husband.

Daniel went through a similar process as **Shadrach, Meshach, and Abednego**. He was thrown into the lion's den for refusing to stop praying to God. He would not bow to the decree of the Medes or the Persians. He would not be influenced by them; instead his actions would influence the whole nation. When God saved Daniel from the den of lions, the Bible records the king's response:

'Then King Darius wrote: To all peoples, nations, and languages that dwell in all the earth: Peace be multiplied to you. I make a decree that in every dominion of my kingdom men must tremble and fear before the God of Daniel.
For He is the living God,
And steadfast forever;
His kingdom is the one which shall not be destroyed,
And His dominion shall endure to the end.
He delivers and rescues,

Positioned to influence

And He works signs and wonders
In heaven and on earth,
Who has delivered Daniel from the power of the lions'
(Daniel 6:25–27).

People will need to be influenced by believers in order to recognise the only true God. How will they be influenced if the believers cower in fear and back down when challenged? I love the answer of the three young men; that God would deliver them, and if even if He did not, they would still not bow. Some people will praise God because they see you being steadfast in your faith even when faced with life-threatening situations. Society places demands on the faith of believers, who have to be strong to withstand the constant onslaught.

The bride of Jesus is under pressure to conform to the standards of this world. Some think doing business means bribing officials for tenders or bribing potential bosses for a promotion. Women pay with their bodies for jobs and promotions. Some believers are tempted to choose the immoral and sinful way of getting ahead in life. Societal values and culture will always put pressure on people. Jesus lived contrary to culture in many areas. He broke cultural standards on the observance of the Sabbath, and would rather heal and help on the Sabbath than bow to the cultural norm of doing nothing on that day.

The Bride of Jesus

He included women in His ministry, contrary to the societal standards of the time which dictated that women should stay at home and take care of the household. Women ministered to His needs, and when the time was right, Jesus entrusted them with the proclamation of His resurrection: *'Then Jesus said to them, "Do not be afraid. Go and tell My brethren to go to Galilee, and there they will see Me"'* (Matthew 28:10).

The bride of Jesus must rise up and be counted. Her presence must be felt in the market place, in the town square and in the boardroom. She has a duty to fund the Kingdom. The Church must be influential in all spheres, and be heard even when no one listens. We cannot measure the impact we have by what we see; but we have what it takes to re-shape the world.

Influence or be influenced!

18
The bride

'He who has the bride is the bridegroom; but the friend of the bridegroom, who stands and hears him, rejoices greatly because of the bridegroom's voice. Therefore this joy of mine is fulfilled'

(John 3:29).

The bride is flanked by bridesmaids and the groom by groomsmen, who together make up the wedding party. There are many others who participate actively in the wedding preparations. The caterer makes sure there is enough tasty food. The decorator makes sure the venue looks stunning. The photographer captures the beauty and specialness of the day in images that will be valued by the family for years.

Yet when the couple stands before the pastor, only the man and the woman take those solemn vows. Only

The Bride of Jesus

these two will be pronounced husband and wife. The bridesmaids, groomsmen, caterer, decorator and photographer will all go home. Then the two become one. Being a part of the wedding does not make the onlookers part of the marriage.

Some of the people attending the wedding may not even have good intentions. Some may be gatecrashers. Some may be passers-by who heard the loud music and ululating and came in to see what was happening. A wedding is exciting to all, even if we do not know the couple marrying.

In like fashion, the gathering of believers is full of people, all of whom participate in some way but not all of whom are part of the bride of Jesus. They walk with the bride, may take care of the bride, and may even give her tips on how to make her wedding day special. But they are not a part of the marriage between Jesus and His followers.

Some are part of the congregation, but have not made a commitment to the bridegroom. They fill the pews and tick the boxes and fill in the form of membership at the local church, but never register in the heavenly Church.

Some are in the Church to deceive and cause strife between the bride and bridegroom. They are troublemak-

The bride

ers. They don't commit to the bridegroom and they don't want others to commit either. They would rather no one got married.

'The pastor is not anointed enough.' 'The pastor does not preach as well as the junior pastor or the elders.' 'The pastor is not handling the finances of the church properly.' 'The number of members is going down.' 'The pastor favours certain people. The brethren are talking about them.' They come to church to complain, and cause division and trouble. When such people open their mouths you wonder if they even know the name of the bridegroom.

Some are there for social reasons. They want to be known as churchgoers, so that they will be buried nicely. Some like the concept of church, but do not have a relationship with Christ. They are there to show off their new cars, to give a huge offering and to be known by the church as the biggest financiers. They are there, filling the pews.

'Enter by the narrow gate; for wide is the gate and broad is the way that leads to destruction, and there are many who go in by it. Narrow is the gate and difficult is the way which leads to life, and there are few who find it' (Matthew 7:13)

The Bride of Jesus

The gate is narrow. Complainers, unbelievers, the bitter, the jealous, the liars, the adulterous and the idolatrous carry baggage, and do not want to put it down in order to meet Christ. They try to get in with baggage, but are unable to fit through that narrow gate. They stand there, holding onto their sins. Some are waiting at the gate for a time when they will hear the trumpet, so that they may drop their baggage and run inside at that point. Unfortunately, they may die at the gate, still holding their baggage.

They are all invited to the feast, as Jesus said in Matthew 22:1–14, but they are not all willing to come. In the parable of the king who invited unwilling guests, the king eventually sent his servants to the highways and byways, to call in as many as they could find, so that the wedding hall could be filled with guests.

The true bride of Jesus sits right alongside the false bride, for *'Let both grow together until the harvest, and at the time of harvest I will say to the reapers, "First gather together the tares and bind them in bundles to burn them, but gather the wheat into my barn"'* (Matthew 13:30).

It is not the responsibility of the bride of Jesus to root out the tares. She must just be aware. She must be careful not to become entangled with the tares lest she loses her distinctiveness. Since human beings are not plants, God has a plan of salvation for us, which the tares

The bride

may receive at any time and so become counted among the wheat.

The end times bring an even more challenging scenario. They bring shepherds who are false and are leading people to eternal damnation. They do mighty miracles, signs and wonders and deceive many. They get their powers from evil forces and because people are seeking signs, these false leaders give them what they want. Jesus would not give signs to those who did not believe His simple message. They were more interested in signs than in truth.

'Many will say to Me in that day, "Lord, Lord, have we not prophesied in Your name, cast out demons in Your name, and done many wonders in Your name?"' (Matthew 7:22).

They prophecy, of course; they will tell you the car you drive, the job you do, the colour of your undergarments. They will tell you hidden things for no good reason. They rarely tell you, 'Repent and be baptised.'

They dance to the drum of need. You need a job, and they dance for you to the tune of jobs and money. You want a wife, and they respond to that. You want a business and they respond to that. They don't tell you that you lack prayer in your life, or that you are sleeping with your neighbour's wife, or that you are practising fraud in

The Bride of Jesus

the workplace. They don't want to lose followers by proclaiming the truth. They stay on safe terrain – tickling the ears of the desperate.

'Beware of false prophets, who come to you in sheep's clothing, but inwardly they are ravenous wolves. You will know them by their fruits. Do men gather grapes from thorn bushes or figs from thistles? ... Therefore by their fruits you will know them' (Matthew 7:15-16, 20).

False prophets have little lasting fruit in their lives. Their works are evil. A false prophet is not false because his prophecies fail – he is false because he poses as a man sent by God, when God has not sent him. So do not judge them on whether their prophecies are accurate. Even witchdoctors will tell you hidden things. The issue is not the message, but the source of the message. They do not produce the fruits of the Spirit. They produce the works of the flesh.

The bride of Jesus may be enticed by these false prophets and pastors because they tell us what we want to hear. You want a job – here, take it! They will not tell you God wants you to minister for two years first, then get a job. They will not tell you that your womb is closed because you take things that don't belong to you, as Abimelech took Abraham's wife.

The bride

When you bring money, and lie about it, they will not ask you, *'Ananias, why has Satan filled your heart to lie to the Holy Spirit and keep back part of the price of the land for yourself? While it remained, was it not your own? And after it was sold, was it not in your own control? Why have you conceived this thing in your heart? You have not lied to men but to God'* (Acts 5:3–4). Why not? Because the money you have brought is a lot and will cover their salaries. Ananias' sin was not in keeping part of the money, but in lying about it, as many lie today about the source of the gifts they bring.

'Now the works of the flesh are evident, which are adultery, fornication, uncleanness, lewdness, idolatry, sorcery, hatred, contentions, jealousies, outbursts of wrath, selfish ambitions, dissensions, heresies, envy, murders, drunkenness, revelries, and the like; of which I tell you beforehand, just as I also told you in time past, that those who practice such things will not inherit the kingdom of God' (Galatians 5:19).

The Church has become a place where truth is concealed for fear of retribution. In some cases, the Church has sold her soul to the laws of the country, and her message is censored. The world does not care about biblical standards, yet far too often the Church is expected to care about worldly standards. You cannot walk into a bar and tell the patrons not to dance in a provocative way

The Bride of Jesus

when they are drunk. You cannot even walk in there and tell them not to waste the money that ought to go to their children. Yet the Church is told not to preach certain messages because the message may offend some people.

Many in the Church also censor their message to the believers inside the church, for fear of offending.

What can be preached then? Only the things that appeal to taste. You will easily find preachers willing to address people's wants and desires, but not their deepest need. People need Jesus, people need salvation, far more than they need a car, a house or a husband. Yet some would rather focus on the passing glory than the eternal glory.

The bride of Jesus will discern this, and ensure that her life is grounded, rooted and bearing fruit.

'But the fruit of the Spirit is love, joy, peace, long-suffering, kindness, goodness, faithfulness, gentleness, self-control. Against such there is no law. And those who are Christ's have crucified the flesh with its passions and desires' (Galatians 5:22-24).

The Church arises as a glorious bride to welcome her husband. The fruit is evident. She may not appeal to most, but she appeals to her husband. Her objective in life is to please the Lord. She is manifesting the Lord. She loves not only the rich, but the poor also. Her love is

The bride

not conditional upon favours being granted, because her love flows from God, who loves the unlovable.

She finds her joy in the Lord, not in tangible things. She is joyful in lack and joyful in plenty. She has come to the point of saying, 'Jesus, you are enough for me.' She knows that in Christ she has all things and lives by the words of Matthew 6:33: *'But seek first the kingdom of God and His righteousness, and all these things shall be added to you.'*

The bride of Jesus is a peacemaker. She is not seeking to settle scores with her enemies. She does not desire to win an argument while losing a sister. She leaves her enemies to God, as instructed by Romans 12:19: *'Beloved, do not avenge yourselves, but rather give place to wrath; for it is written, "Vengeance is Mine, I will repay," says the Lord.'*

The bride seeks the peace of God in His house. She herself has peace in times of trouble for she knows God has everything under control. She knows that weapons may be formed against her, but none will prosper. She therefore does not fret over little things. She is blessed for she is a peacemaker at home, in church, at work and in society.

She understands that love suffers long, and is patient and tolerant. She gives her sister or brother in the Lord space to grow and does not look down on them be-

The Bride of Jesus

cause they are still feeding on milk. She stands on the Word of God even when things take a long time to be resolved. She trusts her Lord.

Her kindness is spoken off, not because she smiles and laughs a lot, but because her deeds speak for themselves. The likes of Dorcas have been multiplied in her; she loves the people of God and takes care of their needs.

When she gives, she gives out of a good heart, not to score points on social media or to expose the poverty of the poor. Her kindness is shown not only to those who believe with her at church, but also to her family. She knows that the Lord said the one who does not take care of her own family is worse than a sinner. She does good whenever the opportunity arises. She is not perfect, but her goodness surpasses her mistakes. She handles issues in a gentle manner, not roughly with the tongue. She will not hurt her brothers or sisters deliberately, but her speech is seasoned with salt.

She is a faithful bride who does not commit harlotry with every manmade god in the world. She is focused on building her relationship with the Lord. She does not doubt Him, but knows He is sufficient. So she does not run after other gods when the answers to her prayers take long to manifest.

The bride

While the world offers her good things, the bride of Jesus exercises self-control. She does not justify addictions and wrong doing as 'natural urges'. She knows what God says concerning the issues of life and she would rather have God help her than blame God for her lack of self-control.

Even during the tribulation, the Lord is certain that His bride will come out as white as snow. *'And I said to him, "Sir, you know." So he said to me, "These are the ones who come out of the great tribulation, and washed their robes and made them white in the blood of the Lamb'* (Revelation 7:14).

'Then I, John, saw the holy city, New Jerusalem, coming down out of heaven from God, prepared as a bride adorned for her husband' (Revelation 21:2).

Are you that bride?

Will you be there when the bridegroom comes

in

all His glory?

Will you be at the wedding feast?

Author's parting words

The Bride of Jesus; this is an intimate topic, the heart of God towards the Church. It was necessary that this book be written. In the same way as my third book, *Dear Girl Child*, I did not plan to write this book, but the Lord had His way. It is a part of my calling to write, and to deliver a message to the Church.

This book is meant to lift up Jesus and place Him at the centre of the heart of the believer, and the congregation.

If you have ever felt unloved, may *The Bride of Jesus* bestow a white robe on you and walk you down the aisle to a waiting bridegroom, whose love never fades. His thoughts are always about us. Because of this great love, He saw fit to die for us.

The Bride of Jesus is my fifth book in hard copy, coming after *Confessions of a Parent*. My first two books, *From the Pit to the Palace: a Prisoner made Governor* and *Victorious Youth* are still in print and touching lives.

My books are available at Kingdom Anchored bookshops, at Exclusive Books in South Africa and online at amazon.com.

The Bride of Jesus

Contact me on email <u>carolnkambule@gmail.com</u>

Website <u>www.kingdomanchored.co.za</u>

www.ingramcontent.com/pod-product-compliance
Lightning Source LLC
Chambersburg PA
CBHW031345040426
42444CB00005B/197